Thirty-Seven Ideas For Business Operation Improvement*

*What Are The Odds You Can Use At Least One?

By:

Ron Parker

ISBN: 978-0615500287

Table of Contents

Acknowledgements

Dr. Charles R. Hobbs created *Time Power*, an insightful approach to Time Management that places *your time and your life* at the center of Time Management.

By continually emphasizing the distinction between the important and the urgent, he teaches how to keep one's highest values as the foundation of decision making. You will see this theme in some of the following articles, and I want to acknowledge the source and its lasting value.

Dr. Hobbs was also inspiring to me as a career role model. When I was first offered an opportunity to teach and consult for business audiences, it was my positive experiences as Dr. Hobbs's student that I wanted to re-create for my own audiences.

James. C. Abbott of Abbott Associates gave me the opportunity to teach and consult with business audiences. I have yet to find productive work that I enjoy more.

Working with James over several years and many projects accounts for a *cross-pollination* of skills as I gained experience and maturity.

I worked with James when he pioneered computer training and consulting for accountants, engineers and executives. When public education caught up and began offering computer training for all, we moved ahead.

*Thirty Seven Ideas For Business Operation Improvement**

Drawing on our engineering, mathematics and science backgrounds, we offered services in Manufacturing and Statistical Quality Control.

When the Deming inspired *quality improvement* impetus morphed into an industry appetite for brand name *quality certification* programs, we re-focused our teaching and coaching on development of new techniques for project and process managers.

As US manufacturing increasingly moved offshore, we turned our attention to the *back office* and to the *service side* of business, including: customer service, accounting operations, case handling, *technology* help desks and call centers.

Had I not met James, I would most likely have confined my consulting to technology projects. I would have missed the diversity of experience and the broad overarching view of operations: from engineering to production, from customer service to the back office.

Finally, this book would not have been possible without the help of my wife, **Trudy**. She has encouraged me for years to collect some of my articles and release them in the form of a book.

She has been a patient reader of early drafts and has helped me to turn the rough drafts of these articles into more polished versions that can be released in book form.

Thank you, Trudy, for helping me to produce this book before the last twilight of print, and its 21st century companion at eBook's dawn.

Introduction

You may have heard the old story of the bar crowd that had been together so long, every joke and tall tale was numbered. "Forty Seven", someone would say; and the crowd would roar with laughter. So the new guy tries. "Twenty Two!", but the crowd doesn't laugh. Instead, they are uncomfortably silent. Finally, an old-timer offers some advice. "It wasn't the joke kid. It was how you told it."

The bar story always makes me smile because it rings true. I had a childhood friend who could always make me laugh with "It came out of the bricks." instead of "It came out of nowhere." Of course for this short-hand humor to work, "you had to be there." If you catch yourself making something harder than it needs to be, you can just say, "Doh!" and everyone who has seen *The Simpsons* instantly understands your frustration.

I wrote these articles as an invitation for you to "be there", to join me at work for just a couple of minutes at a time. Each article represents a condensed experience or insight that made a positive difference for a company or for an individual.

The variety in subject matter reflects the diversity of assignments that I have been fortunate to receive over the last twenty years. I have learned so much by *crossing disciplines,* and I hope *you* can find value in stories outside your own specialty.

Therefore, no attempt has been made to group the manufacturing lessons, the statistics, the call center experiences or the leadership stories. The order of these articles is more or less in the order they were written.

Each reader brings a personal background to written material. You may find a particular point profound and someone else may consider it trivial or confusing. My hope is that out of these thirty seven ideas you will find at least one that can really make a difference for you.

1: Managing 10 or 1000

What are the similarities and differences of managing a few or many? What advice would you give to the newly promoted? What will be similar? What is going to change?

THE SIMILARITIES

Managers always work with and through the cooperation of others. Management at any level counts on a proper organization of work and on the competencies of others to be successful. Management of many simply exaggerates and makes this fact more obvious.

Technology may enhance our power to speak, and we have the means to issue directives to a billion people, but technology cannot make it possible to *listen* to a billion individuals. We will never listen to, read an email or a book, or see news stories or movies featuring most of the people alive on the planet today.

*Do the math! 15 minutes listening only once to a person multiplied by 100,000 people takes **12 years** at a dedicated 40 hours per week!*

It is a proper organizational structure and division of labor that makes it possible for leaders of few or many *to listen to the right things at the right time.*

If the organizational structure is sound, all managers deal with approximately the same number of direct reports and peers. I discussed this with a Parris Island Marine Colonel who put it this way:

> *"The Corp develops leadership throughout the organization, training individuals to step forward into the next tier of responsibility. Although I am responsible for more than a thousand soldiers, I spend most of my time working closely with about a dozen other people, and so does a squad leader."*

THE DIFFERENCES

As managers are promoted to higher and higher levels of responsibility, there will be *two key differences*:

1. What is directly perceivable or self-evident to the junior manager becomes increasingly abstract at higher levels. The reverse is also true! Each must think about what the other simply sees.

The view from thirty thousand feet is a metaphor often used to dismiss the CEO's perspective for being blind to the so-called facts on the ground, but the view from *four* feet has weaknesses as well. The fact is, from the two perspectives, each observer sees what the other must understand abstractly.

2. With each promotion, a manager's role in an organization involves more strategic decisions and fewer tactical decisions.

RISK BECOMES REAL TO THE MANAGER OF MANY

It is difficult for many entry-level managers to incorporate risk-analysis in their decision-making. Risk is *so* abstract that it doesn't seem to possess the power of reality.

Suppose spare tires were options when you purchased your first car. "Take it." The dealer would advise. "You'll need it, *if you have a flat!*" Suppose you don't buy the spare, and in ten years of driving you never had the predicted flat tire. *What conclusions would you draw?*

Good management practices in small organizations often target the management and reduction of risk. If risks are small, good habits often go un-rewarded and bad habits often go unpunished.

For example, a capability study may calculate an increased risk of scrap if a process is operated while SPC analysis shows the process is out of control. Some managers choose to flaunt the statistical warnings and press on, avoiding scrap on their watch by luck of the draw.

The manager of many is subject to the discipline of large numbers. The abstract risk in small numbers approaches a tangible certainty as the numbers increase. The principles underlying actions will have many more opportunities to manifest their consequences.

This calls for a small revision of an old warning, "Be careful what you ask for: in small numbers you *risk* getting it, in large numbers **you will!**"

This *large number* effect applies to the many unlikely but possible adversities and tragedies of life and work. For example, the manager of many will more likely encounter difficult employee issues. Many managers of ten may, with luck, avoid a *problem employee* decision for a year or even five. The biggest risk for the newly promoted is the failure to deal directly, rationally, and decisively with the unpleasant when it inevitably arises.

EVERYDAY WORK IS ABSTRACT TO THE MANAGER OF MANY.

It becomes impossible to understand a very large business by just looking. The work must be conceptualized.

Properly done, process dependencies and management metrics tell the manager of ten what they are seeing with their own eyes. For the manager of many, conceptual tools are the only way to grasp the current state of the business.

The newly promoted manager must strive to master the appropriate tools of their position and not simply imitate the motions of their predecessor. They also need to learn to detect flawed legacy reports that are actually floating abstractions; i.e. conceptual fantasies that *claim* to describe the current state of the business, but actually have no connection to reality.

HIGHER MANAGEMENT DECISIONS ARE INCREASINGLY STRATEGIC.

With each promotion, a manager's role in an organization involves more strategic decisions and fewer tactical decisions. Some reflection on the division of labor in decision-making is in order. Are you ultimately responsible for the commercial success of a product or product family? Do you manage the supporting engineering and project departments necessary to build and modify the processes of your business? Or, are you expected to run the existing processes as correctly and consistently as possible?

The top leadership of an organization is responsible for its *Policy*, the integrating idea of what the company will be and what it will do. *Strategic* decision makers are responsible for goals, the evaluation of risk, and for the identification and operational funding of necessary project objectives and process capabilities.

Within the constraints of operational funding, *Tactical* decision makers are responsible for a) the correct and consistent execution of projects, b) the correct and consistent operations of business processes.

A FINAL PIECE OF ADVICE TO THE NEWLY PROMOTED MANAGER

It is a mistake to think that your last job has prepared you for your new job. This is only true if you are committed to lifelong learning.

The competencies you have perfected in your last job are perfect for just that - your *last* job. The policy of learning something new every day is increasingly important with each promotion. It can help you beat the Peter Principle - *the pattern of promotion beyond productiveness.*

2: How Do You Know...

WHERE TO START

As an improvement consultant, I am asked, *"How do you know where to start? How do you zero in on a problem area with a high likelihood that sustainable improvements can be made?"*

The answer is two parts. There is the obvious and familiar starting strategy - *follow the money*, and there is a *trade secret* of rapid improvement.

Following the money simply means auditing the critical path - the sequence of tasks that must be executed in order for the business to get paid. I look for the things you might expect along this path, capacities & bottlenecks, first pass yields, proper tools for the job and so on.

The *trade secret* of rapid improvement is this:

> *Look for indecision, uncertainty, and trial & error behavior.*

Now, let me stress that this is not the problem. It is a symptom or warning flag, an X that marks exactly the spot on the business critical path where one should dig for treasure. Improvement is not simply achieved by squashing disagreement and reckless boldness pretending to be certainty.

I have tracked these clues through all kinds of processes: call centers, accounting operations, technology infrastructure and manufacturing. One of the clearest illustrations that trial and error behavior denotes a serious process problem is the story of one client's metal machining operation.

THE STORY OF THE EIGHT STATION

The plant had everything from low end computer controlled cutting equipment (CNC machines) to high end finishing equipment designed for better than 100 millionths of an inch tolerances.

The natural interest of the engineers was the complex CNC devices, and the high precision finishing tools, but in this facility there was a *big payoff* opportunity that had not been discovered.

An inexpensive series of low tech workstations prepared every single metal casting before they went into the CNC or finish-work processes. The centerpiece of this line was called the *eight station*. Designed for low cost and maximum throughput, the heart of this workstation was a turntable on which eight un-worked metal castings were placed at forty-five degree intervals.

The table would make a 1/8th turn, and each of seven machining stations would simultaneously make their specific cuts. Station #8 was for the operator who loaded and unloaded parts.

It was soon obvious to me that this particular operation was a den of confusion. The operators called it, *the machine from hell. "Only Johnny can set it up, and it takes hours.", they said.*

As I watched, I quickly saw why the machine was so difficult to set up. Eight fixtures for holding parts must be bolted onto the turntable. They could be placed too close or too far from the center of the table. They could be placed too far to the left or to the right. Two degrees of freedom times eight fixtures equals sixteen different adjustments that must be exactly right.

There was more. The operators had to unbolt and lever the machining stations into position. Seven movable machining stations meant fourteen more dimensions to the problem. There were a grand total of 30 independent but interrelated dimensional adjustments that had to be brought into harmony before the machine was set correctly.

I watched as Johnny, the best operator in the house, struggled for hours to get all the pieces of this machine into position. Tweaking the setup by trial and error, one adjustment always led to a dozen re-adjustments.

A trial run meant wasting raw material by making sample cuts that were sent to the measurement lab for evaluation. It was usually fatigue and an urgent demand for production that forced him to surrender the cause and actually attempt to produce a product.

THE SOLUTION

I took a little time to think about the problem. How should the setup of this machine be handled? When I thought I had the answer, I went back to Johnny.

"Tell me" I asked, "Is there anything on this machine you won´t move to make a correct setup?"

Johnny answered, "Well, the engineers told me that I should try not to move the stations on the left and right of the operator position. They didn´t know why. I tried to leave them alone but I´ve had to move them anyhow."

His answer confirmed my suspicions. The machine's designer had intended that two of the workstations, together with the center of the turntable, form a perfect ninety-degree angle.

Those three points would establish the absolute reference frame from which every component could easily and systematically be placed in its one and only one correct position.

Once this *carpenter´s square* had been broken, the machine could no longer be set up with certainty. There was no longer one and only one place to position any component.

The solution was:

1. Re-establish the permanent location of the two stations on either side of the operator by precision measurement.

2. Teach the operators that the setup process must be remembered as an ABC sequence that must be followed carefully and in order.

   a) The built-in 90-degree reference angle must never be altered. It shows *where to exactly place fixtures.*

   b) Fixtures are systematically placed on the turntable underneath the two workstations on either side of the operator. The table is turned, and then all fixtures determine the *one and only one place* for the remaining five workstations.

   c) The remaining five workstations are positioned last, after every fixture has been placed on the table and carefully aligned with the immovable workstations on either side of the operator.

There were some optional elements to this improved setup, but it was no longer trial and error. Instead, it was now a consistent process with a predictable duration and a certain outcome.

THE REST OF THE STORY

The rest of the story has to answer one big question.

What drove the operators to break the rule and move the two forbidden machine stations?

First of all, no one in the plant truly understood the significance of those two stations on either side of the operator.

*What Are The Odds you Can Use At Least One?

A perfect 90 degree angle establishes a repeatable frame of reference for measurement.

Although operators were directed to never move two of the machining workstations, they later received directions that created a conflict.

A reliance on obedience to procedure combined with an absence of process knowledge is a risky thing. If there are two orders to obey, and the orders appear to conflict, then what will happen?

Without process knowledge, the outcome is left to chance.

The conflict was created by a fundamental flaw in management´s *setup* decision rules.

How do you know when a setup is correct? The flawed decision rule said, *"A sample cut must be made and compared to specifications."*

The proper decision rule is, "*When you have audited and are certain that you have adhered to every aspect of a correct setup process.*" It is engineering´s responsibility to see that a correct process will produce the intended product.

In this plant, *setup* was deemed to be wrong if a sample part failed a QC measurement check. (Imagine a math teacher that only checks answers and not *how* the answer was computed.)

This plant's *setup* policy was additionally flawed because of the assumption that a single selected sample will always be average.

Questionable measurement precision in this plant compounded the problem, and drove operators to a point where they felt they had no alternative but to break the machine to gain setup approval.

FOOTNOTE FOR THE MECHANICAL ENGINEER:

Pinning this machine was not the solution, and only added constraints that made it impossible to correct the problem.

After the reference angle was broken, engineering had tried to sort out the mess by welding positioning pins to the turntable. They deprived the setup operator of the ability to make necessary adjustments and therefore made matters worse.

3: Dilbert

There are two sides to an old argument, and I have heard both many times and in many circumstances.

The debate usually begins like this: Dilbert, who is a salesman, agent, operator, mechanic, accountant, engineer, programmer or some other soldier of business, puts the discussion in play.

> *"What a disaster in the making! Our new boss has no clue about the details of this business. No doubt they teach them in school that managers need not know the business in order to run it. This happened at the last place I worked, and they closed in less than a year. Better get your resumes ready!"*

The other side of the coin is usually argued by a generalist manager who, by their protests, identify themself as the boss that Dilbert is talking about. They want to defend their contribution to a company´s success.

> *"Well, I was hired to turn around XYZ, Inc and I did it in less than a year! I re-organized (or: re-prioritized, re-scheduled, re-located, re-incentivized) the organization with retreats/goals/Monday staff meetings/MBO/metrics. I don´t have to know what I am measuring to interpret the data."*

> *"There is a place for the professional manager. Why, just look what happens to a company when they put an accountant, engineer or a salesman in charge!"*

We have all seen situations or heard stories that would seem to support both positions. This leads us to think that there might be an underlying condition, a hidden *if* that tilts a case study to one position or the other.

WHAT IS IT ABOUT THE ORGANIZATION THAT NEEDS FIXING?

In some businesses, operations flaws are minor, and the organization needs a cohesive vision. Such a business has well-designed processes and a tactical workforce that understands the business product.

Without direction, the best tactical teams often lack focus. A new manager may remedy this problem without spending a lot of time in the nuts and bolts. The perfect analogy is a parked car with no place to go, its finely tuned engine running, waiting on a driver and destination.

Competent tacticians who are quite comfortable with *tactical decisions* are often paralyzed by *strategic choices*.

When an issue is purely tactical, a *T ledger* can be made of pros and cons or a clever programmer can code a decision tree. Even if some of the inputs are probabilistic (e.g. *40% chance of project delay due to weather*), it is still possible to reduce the issue to a data-driven solution.

When confronted with *choices* which require weighing values and qualitative risks or picking one of three alternatives, many tacticians find themselves in a *Hamlet loop*. They will debate the *"To Be or Not To Be"* of the issue endlessly and without resolution.

After exhausting everyone with all of their *reasons for*, they can return from a break with a hundred and one *reasons against;* suddenly opposing the position they just held before lunch.

One successful turn-around manager said, "*My new staff had fourteen different visions of the company mission.*" His success depended on getting the organization to focus and not upon learning the details of each technician's job.

But what if the organization is not the finely maintained and tuned race-car looking for a driver? To continue the analogy, what if the car has not been maintained? What if parts have been removed and not replaced because they were too much trouble? How do you make an operation *right*, and *then* make it better?

EVENTUALLY, MANAGEMENT NEEDS TO GET INTO THE DETAILS

I´m wary of the turn-around experts who brag that they can **always** *move the numbers* without knowing the operation. Many organizations in trouble have problems that go deeper than motivation, vision and focus.

Sometimes managers fool themselves. They think improvements have been made, and they haven't. A problem *seems* to disappear only to pop up somewhere else.

I know (and can uncover) most of the tricks to *transfer* costs from the business to the customer or to the employee, from the P&L to the balance sheet, from one department or plant to another, and from the short term to the long term. Such *Zero*

Thirty Seven Ideas For Business Operation Improvement*

Sum changes to a business do not improve an operation, and usually cause harm.

A further complication is that many traditional performance metrics are lagging indicators and can temporarily move in the wrong direction during periods of transition. I have two *real life cases* that I have used in training classes where operation´s service level statistics temporarily became better as customer service got *worse*.

Managers who do not understand their business processes are terrified of this transition and often say, "I´m scared to run the business right!"

Eventually, all managers **must** develop an understanding of the details of their business operation. Those managers fortunate enough to inherit a capable tactical organization will eventually need to turn their attention to *sustainment*. Those who inherit an operation with incapable processes need details as a *prerequisite* to focus and vision.

As I have said in **Management Philosophy,** "You need not be a surgeon to discuss *brain surgery*, but you should at least be able to define *brain* and *surgery*. If it is true that you can´t effectively manage without measuring, you surely can´t manage what you cannot define."

4: Let's Not And Say We Did

"If you attend my class" the professor said, "You should be able to pass the test." The law students in the class perked up immediately.

"What do you mean by *attendance?*" they asked. "If I arrive late and leave early, is that ok? What about sick days? Can I tape the class? Does community service count?"

It amazes me to see such effort expended in a quest for *compliance.* Instead of accepting that *attendance means attendance,* the legalistic mind envisions collecting up and cashing in any and all behaviors, credits and frequent flier coupons that will earn the check mark of compliance.

"I met the attendance requirements. I did what you said. Why didn´t I pass?" they will ask.

The answer, the honest truth is that when it came to attendance, this crowd was desperately looking for a way to not attend, and yet claim that they did.

MUDDLE MANAGEMENT

It is in the work place where this attitude really concerns me. In the best schools, students pass when they master the material. Attendance and grades are not a matter of compliance but of demonstrated performance.

Thirty Seven Ideas For Business Operation Improvement*

Alumni of what I call the *Let's not and say we did* school of management turn up at all levels of business, and are the principal impediment to operation improvement.

Muddle Management will declare scheduled meetings to have been held even if no one shows up. They will pronounce operators trained if the company has purchased an instructional video.

Project tasks will be marked as completed not because the work has been done, but because their scheduled time has past. To these *muddle managers*, a Quality Initiative means certifications, awards or some other quality compliance check mark.

ROOT CAUSE

Ideally, the decision support function in a business provides a *complete and clear picture* of the current state of the business. Most internal reporting and analysis does not even approach this ideal.

Instead, metrics are typically *subverted into a complete and clear picture of what managers should be* **paid**. Although we may intend to award salaries, bonuses and promotions based on performance, the result is often that *compliance* is rewarded.

If managers are bonused for *checking off* three quality improvement and two cost savings initiatives, then it is only natural for a muddle manager to think, "How can I qualify?"

Misguided metrics and incentives can divert management attention from performance to compliance. Once the precedent has been set, it is very difficult to turn metrics that reward compliance back to their proper role of monitoring process health and product performance.

The *ask the customer* approach often taken by programmers results in automated *metric* reports that reinforce this negative business culture.

SOLUTION

To grow a performance oriented culture, you must start by revisiting what constitutes excellent operations performance.

For tactical management, excellence is the correct and consistent operation of facilities. For strategic management and engineering, it is capacities, capabilities and costs.

Metrics then need to reflect the *current state of the business* and provide guidance for managers on how to improve. Great metrics are designed around *Better Decisions, Better Products and Lower Costs,* not bonus plans!

5: Cost-Benefit Analysis - Part One

John, the new salesman, was excited about his new company car. His boss would spend over $130,000 on the top of the line luxury vehicle. Plus, the company maintenance team was responsible for the entire motor pool. "We Keep Them Running" was the shop motto.

Precisely at 3000 miles, he took the car to Jack, the maintenance supervisor.

"What's that you are doing, Jack?" he asked.

"Taking off the air filter. It'll only get dirty, and the car runs fine without it.", Jack said. "That muffler's got to go too. It will be nothing but a bucket of rust in a few years – a real maintenance nightmare."

"As for those lug nuts on the tires, you don't need all of them, and it saves us time when we pull the wheels and check the brakes." Jack smiled. "After all, we don't want you going out of here with brakes that don't work!"

John stuttered, "But, but, the engineers who built the car…"

Jack interrupted. "Oh, engineers don't know everything. After all, it's our job to 'keep them running.' Don't worry, after a PM we always have parts left over, but almost everybody drives out of here!"

John, our salesman, couldn't wait to tell his boss. "You won't believe what is going on down in the motor pool."

His boss replied, "I've just seen the report. Isn't it great! They have cut the number of spare parts they need to inventory, reduced the labor hours per preventative maintenance, and cut the PM budget 20%!"

"But look what they have done to the cars! They always stall and have to be cranked again at stoplights. They sound terrible, and they don't steer properly."

"You stop at stop lights anyway – no time lost there. You're here on time today aren't you?" John's boss said. 'Tell you what, if you feel so strongly about this, write up a cost-benefit analysis and prove the maintenance guys are wrong, and we'll consider it."

John took out a piece of paper. "Miles per gallon", he started. "No. Not enough money. How about reliability? Hmmm. Not enough data – maybe in a couple of years. But wait! There won't be anything to *compare* to!"

"Ok." He thought. "How about that engineering textbook? No. They'll say 'It's fine in theory, but…' Oh! This is hopeless!"

And he was right!

…to be continued…

6: Urgency, Procrastination & Risk

"Look Mom! I *un-peeled* all of the bananas for you!" This was a classic Dennis the Menace cartoon. Dennis was standing on a chair and the counter top was covered in banana peels. Dennis's mom was standing with her hands to her face in dismay.

Urgency can be manipulated, accelerated, manufactured. Like bananas, a lot of things keep for a relatively long time unopened and un-peeled. When the wrapper comes off ahead of time one must act quickly or suffer loss.

Time is the opportunity for action. Specifically, it is the opportunity to think and choose one's best action. Dennis's mom no longer has time on her side. In fact, the opposite is true. She has only minutes to decide how to best use several days worth of bananas.

In the name of motivation, *Banana Peelers* may often use manufactured urgency in a manipulative manner. They contrive an *act or lose* situation to get people to do what they want, when they want it done.

When *expediting pressure* is applied judiciously, it can be an effective management tool. However, for some people this is a *preferred behavior* and their habitual attempts to stampede action will provoke resentment and rebelling behavior – opposite results!

Remember, if every task is *As Soon As Possible*, or *Top Priority*, then the whole strategy of prioritization collapses. One achieves focus and control by *choosing* where one's efforts will be most effective.

The opposite of the *banana peeler* is the procrastinator. Chronic procrastinators will buy bananas, put off peeling them, and then throw them away once they are rotten. All decisions pertaining to their best use are thereby avoided.

If a person is indecisive, they will also be a *chronic* procrastinator, but judicious procrastination can also be an effective management tool.

Some tasks are legitimately postponed to a more appropriate time. I never perform any kind of irreversible computer housekeeping late in the day or when I am tired. I always postpone that kind of maintenance to a time where I am sure to be clear headed and less prone to mistakes.

Our capacity to evaluate, choose and act is finite. At any point in time there can be more issues in play than our finite minds can process. Because of this, we focus on the most vital issues and procrastinate other tasks indefinitely, or *As Late As Possible*.

Banana Peeling and Procrastination are the complementary vices of manufacturing urgency and indefinitely postponing decisions. An excess of either as a preferred behavior cannot be simply dismissed as a *management style*, but the judicious use of **ASAP** and **ALAP** can be a legitimate tool for the mitigation of risk.

7: Cost-Benefit Analysis - Part Two

The academic intent of a business case, and particularly a cost-benefit analysis, is to document and provide context for the choices and decisions made in an organization. In practice, it is a poorly understood and misused tool. As a result, many business cases are nothing more than obligatory and weightless rationalizations.

To unravel this issue, let us first start with a common situation.

Sue says to her boss, *"Jay. Why don't we buy tape from CarolinaTapeCo.com? Their web site makes it easy!"*

Jay thinks... *"Didn't we switch vendors about six months ago? What a hassle! We are a fifty-million-dollar-a-year operation and it took Jake in accounting 12 hours of paperwork, phone calls and a little begging to get NET 10 terms. Didn't we sign a long term contract? What if the tape isn't as good? Is this new vendor for real, or are they going to be out of business next year?"*

...And then Jay says,

"That's an interesting idea, Sue. Why don't you write up a business case."

Now, even if Sue anticipates all of the issues and objections that her boss might have, and if she researches each of the issues and prepares a risk-weighted cost-benefit analysis with contingencies; will this company be better as a result? Or will Sue, a productive member of the organization, be sidelined for a week or two?

THE FIRST MISTAKE

The first mistake that companies make is to use *business case* methodology in a piecemeal fashion, hoping it will somehow reveal the *right* course of action.

In fact, business decision-making is on-going. Earlier *precedent* decisions condition later decisions. Properly designed business cases document the decision-making process and preserve what the organization has learned.

The first business case should be relatively easy.

1. We need tape! (AcmeTape will ship today!)

Then some time later,

2. XYZTapeCo will ship tape and invoice us! (No more CODs!)

The next development and the next business case might be:

3. XYZTapeCo is often out of stock! (EmersonTapeCo will guarantee delivery if we sign a one year contract!)

And finally,

> *4. EmersonTapeCo's delivery is no better than XYZTapeCo. (The decision to commit to a one year contract is rescinded.)*

By the time Sue comes along with what may be a better product or vendor, we should have a context with four precedents established— what we purchased and why!

Sue's boss can then say: *"Why don't you look back over our business cases for **tape**, and write up why you think this new vendor will be better."*

ORGANIZATION

I suspect most organizations cannot readily lay their hands upon relevant precedent business cases. Most likely, these *compliance* documents are buried in the back of a project file or even shredded once the case-maker has been safely promoted.

Employees like Sue do not have a history and context of how the status-quo came to be, they only have the status-quo. When the status-quo has been profitable, or at least tolerable, it is almost impossible to make a case for change.

To risk *something that works* for something better is a hard sell. *"If it ain't broke...."*, will be the reaction, and the *perfect* business case will be tabled *"for further study"*.

THE SECOND MISTAKE

Some matters do not lend themselves to the *business case* approach at all. An example with extremes should illustrate this.

Suppose Sue looks back at the history of tape vendor decisions and sets herself the task of preparing a **T** ledger of pros and cons for a new tape vendor. At the bottom, she draws a line and the weight of evidence favors a change in vendors.

Her boss approves, and then says, "*I like this approach! Can you make another* **T** *ledger for our managers' retreat? Give us the pros and cons on: "Why we should be honest with our customers."*"

Knowledge that we bring into our business in the form of principles is not validated or disputed with the **T** ledger.

Principles are careful summations of significant causal relationships. (e.g. "*Dishonesty leads to business failure.*") Principles of sound business operations will always *trump* any tactical **T** ledger or cost-benefit analysis.

This is the answer that John, our salesman in **Part One** of this article, was looking for. Any sort of *cost-benefit* justification in favor of the absurd maintenance shortcuts is flawed, and should be rescinded on the grounds that those shortcuts are flagrantly contrary to sound business principles.

The catch for salesman John, of course, is that he must be able to articulate those business principles!

8: Six-Sigma Caveat

Six-Sigma anywhere in the title of a book, article or website is guaranteed to draw attention. Businesses are urgently asking *"What's our sigma?"*, knowing only that "6" is supposedly good, and unsure of what is bad. If you don't know a +6 from a -12 sigma then read this now, and don't make a *Six-Sigma* mistake.

RISK

When most people talk about 4, 5 or 6 *sigmas*, they are often talking casually about a statistical calculation known as a Z-Score. For decision-making purposes, this is typically *the next to the last step in calculating something that is actually useful*! That last step in the calculation is an estimate of risk.

Several years ago, a client asked me to predict the future! He said, "I have two welding work stations. They are each outfitted to perform the same kind of work. Each has been known to occasionally produce an improper weld. What can I expect in the future? What should I do? "

Pause, and realize that this is not the same as simply extrapolating the historical performance. If you have never received a traffic ticket, does that mean we forecast 0% chance of tickets in the future? Certainly not! An estimate of *traffic ticket risk* would have to take into account many things, including how and where you drive.

Any calculation of risk is a *chain of reasoning* with critical assumptions that must be checked at each link in the chain.

What Are The Odds you Can Use At Least One?

Failure to do so produces results that are worse than wrong; they are arbitrary! (Wrong answers can be fixed but arbitrary answers cannot!)

In this chain of calculation, the prelude to the final answer is the Z-Score (Sigma) calculation. From this answer the final answer, risk, can be determined.

After comprehensive research which included a visit to the welding operation, this is the kind of report that I made:

I expect that Welder#1 will fail almost 32% of the time, whereas Welder#2 will fail only 4.5% of the time. To save money immediately *without additional capital spending*, take the following actions:

1. Don't ever use Welder#1 unless you have so much demand that you have no choice.

2. If you need 1000 units welded, schedule 1048 if you use machine #2 and schedule 1465 if you use machine #1.

3. Make sure that your calculations of costs and profitability take into account the 48 (or 465) units of scrap and re-work. Modify your capital investment, product line, sales & pricing decisions accordingly.

4. If you *do* invest in replacing or refurbishing this equipment, spend the money on #1 for increased *capacity* or on #2 for increased *precision.*

I DON'T WANT MY SIGMA, I WANT TO KNOW RISK!

Knowledge of the *odds* followed up with quick action *can make a business more profitable immediately!* We can negotiate better contracts, make smarter scheduling decisions and so on.

A Sigma does not help us do this unless 1) it is calculated in a credible fashion, and 2) we complete the last step in calculation by determining risk.

SHORT-CUTS DON'T WORK

Have you had anyone offer to figure your *Sigma* from your scrap report? *"Last month you had 5% scrap, so your Sigma is approximately 2."* they say.

You might ask, *"And...what good is knowing this?"* Well, someone might *try* to estimate your *risk* of scrap from the Sigma of 2, but the estimate would be wrong! The math would lead you to (*No surprise!*) 5%!

Their mysterious Sigma calculation merely equates your recent scrap rate to risk. (Remember traffic tickets?) To anyone who really understands risk as a consideration in decision-making, this is an appalling equivocation.

LEVEL OF RISK IS STRATEGIC

Establishing an acceptable level of risk for today and then choosing the means by which you achieve that level are strategic decisions. There is no single right answer for all companies.

Many businesses are quite profitable with a scrap rate of 5 per hundred, others would be broke at a rate of 5 per ten thousand. Hog farming and medical device manufacturing have considerably different levels of acceptable risk.

You can lower your risk of scrap by primarily tactical (operational) means, as my welding example illustrates. You may also lower risk of defective product by spending capital dollars on technology.

However, if your operation could not run the old technology correctly and consistently, then they probably won't do better with new technology.

WHAT IS SIX SIGMA?

Although everything that allegedly has a connection to business improvement, quality, productivity and clean living has tried to take a position under the *Six Sigma* tent, *Six Sigma* is simply a particular strategic method for managing risk.

Think about our welding machine again. A *Z-Score of 2* implies a failure rate of just under 5% or a welding success rate of 95% .

If one weld was required to complete a product, then 95% of the yield from the welding process could be shipped to customers.

Suppose that three successful welds are required. If one failure makes a bad product, then only 86% (*95% x 95% x 95%*) of the yield from welding can be shipped! If 10 welds are required, the yield is less than 60%!

Motorola is usually credited with originating the *Six-Sigma* strategy. Their goal was internal process success rates that would guarantee a very reliable finished product.

In electronics manufacturing, hundreds and thousands of sequential successes are required to make a successful product. A single failure of a single component can render the entire product useless.

Motorola calculated that if complex products were to work in spite of the enormous number of points of potential failure, then the Z-Scores of internal processes would have to be about six. This process engineering standard became known as *Six-Sigma*.

Motorola made a strategic business decision to intentionally over-engineer key processes and they profited from it. But remember, the goal is to identify and manage risk. There are many strategic and tactical options to that end.

AVOIDING SIX-SIGMA MISTAKES

Before you jump on the Six-Sigma bandwagon, consider the following:

First, remember that the original Six-Sigma was a strategic directive to engineering and not to operations. It establishes an extremely low level of risk as an engineering goal in the development of manufacturing processes.

Over-engineering is not the only means of risk reduction. Your maximum benefit per dollar may be found in the improved operation and management of existing processes.

Second, *Six-Sigma*, and the level of risk that it implies, is not a magic number. It may not be right for you. Are you engaged in Rocket Science or Hog Farming?

How are you measuring scrap or defect? Do you count the billion ticks each second of a computer clock as a billion successes if it works, or as a single failure if it does not?

Third, Get objective help if you want to baseline your present levels of risk. There are countless ways to err in the estimation of risk.

With all of the attention *Six Sigma* garners, there is tremendous pressure on in-house Quality Departments to produce a number that will be *acceptable*, even if the means by which that number is concocted are worse than wrong.

Fourth, Remember that the goal is to manage risk and improve profitability. There are alternatives to an engineering/capital spending binge.

Remember, "*If all you know is a hammer, the whole world looks like a nail.*" Learn about alternatives that have roles for product engineering, process engineering, quality, training, operations and management.

9: How Will We Ever Replace Joe?

We try to design and operate business processes in such a way that new workers can smoothly step into a role or change roles, and continue to deliver the values that customers expect. This does not mean that people are simply interchangeable cogs or a generic commodity that management supplies as an input to the process.

When a good employee leaves, there is inevitably a sense of loss. Since every individual is unique, their contribution to work and to an organization is going to be different than anyone else.

In a benevolent work environment, each new employee brings unexpected capabilities to the workplace that are essentially freebies. These upside surprises sometimes reward the company directly in the form of an unanticipated sale or a cost savings, and sometimes the benefits are intangible in the form of greater team motivation, morale, loyalty, and so on.

Joe, lets say - has a knack for fixing the copy machine. Anne never needs to look up zip codes. Sam can do things in an hour with Excel that might take others two or three hours.

Of course, the reverse is also true. Every employee has the potential to introduce an unexpected drag on the organization. Karen has a sick mother and sometimes misses work. Rick is moody. etc. Steve commutes over 30 miles and has occasionally been made late by unpredictable traffic.

I think everyone is quite aware of these basic facts once attention has been placed upon them. What may not be so obvious is how these issues cloud judgment in the hiring decision.

The recruiting committee will often prepare a filter in the form of a job ad beginning like this: **"Seeking an individual with aptitude and experience in customer service."**

Someone will note that the team always routed warranty issues to Joe as he was more patient with complaining customers. So **"Warranty experience a must!"** is added.

Anne and Sam are rumored to be *looking* so we tack on: **"Advanced spreadsheet skills, a keen memory and mechanical aptitude is a plus."**

Next, while thinking about the negative side of the ledger and trying to formulate a selective but fair criteria - we finish off with: **"Must have a strong work ethic and have a record of punctuality. Preference given to a local applicant."**

Now the motivation behind constructing such a filter is to find **The One.** Although we may consciously reject this, our behavior is actually causing us to seek out the status quo. Even though we can never literally replace Joe we are apparently going to try.

The deal killer is when someone realizes that Joe was the in-house expert on the *ACME AMAZING SOFTWARE PACKAGE FOR Wonderful Customer Service.* So we add to our job requirements: **"Applicant must be familiar with AASPFWCS".** We assume, I suppose, that if you don't even know what the heck the acronym is, you probably don't qualify.

This going nowhere ad then has a boat anchor strapped to it by the eternal optimist on the search committee who imagines that there will be hundreds of equally qualified applicants. **"BS Required. Advanced degree preferred."**

Now, applicants may certainly apply if the salary is right. If they want the job badly enough, they may be willing to try to be Joe with a touch of Anne or Sam, and not themselves.

The fundamental flaw is in how we define our hiring objective. When a great employee like Joe leaves our company, we need to be able to look them in the eye and say, "Joe. We'll find someone to do your job, but we are never going to be able to replace you."

10: The Threshold Of Perception

You may have never heard of or thought about a notion like *The Threshold of Perception*. In fact, for thousands of years this idea would have been inaccessible to all but a few people. In order to grasp the threshold, one must see the threshold *move*!

There are things that are too small for the human eye to see, but they exist. When one has seen a magnifying glass *push back* the threshold, the principle is established. It is then easy to imagine that increases in magnification will reveal still more unseen things.

Vision, like all of the senses, is constrained in many dimensions. There are things that are too small, too large, too distant, too close, too slow or too fast to see. There are colors of perception that we can directly experience only with the aid of technology.

Fortunately, direct experience is not the only tool at our disposal. Think, for example, of a Sherlock Holmes who can deduce the likely height and weight of an unseen individual from the stride and depth of footprints.

In business, even our engineers sometimes forget about the threshold and act contrary to good statistical evidence because they don't hear or see anything!

45

Thirty Seven Ideas For Business Operation Improvement*

One client was using automated machinery to bubble pack its small product, and about 1% of the finished goods was mangled scrap. The company was profitable with scrap rates below 2%, but an aggressive manager wanted to know why his machines would occasionally fail.

A time series study showed that at particular points in time there were slight variances in finished product weight. These variations were negligible with regard to the product's performance, but they signaled the presence of causes and their effects that were below the threshold of perception.

We correlated the variances to a sloppy overuse of a powder lubricant, and the plant engineers laughed. "Haven't you ever heard of *Momentum!*", they said. "Do you seriously believe that a little of this light powder can have the slightest impact on this heavy stainless steel conveyor and the heavy duty electric motor that pulls it."

"Just look", they said. "The conveyor is sweeping away the tiny amounts of excess powder!"

Nevertheless, operations took our advice to heart and eliminated *all* of the scrap with two new additions to their knowledge of a correct process. One of those was a change in the way the powder reservoir was filled.

The gallon-sized powder scoop was replaced with a one quart size. With tools that were commensurate to the manual task of scooping powder and adding it to a machine reservoir, excess powder was eliminated and so was scrap.

The exciting and relevant *rest of the story* is what happened next. A gadget salesman made a call on the plant. He offered a slow motion video technology similar to that used in nature photography and he demonstrated his product on a packaging machine conveyor.

Time was slowed by a factor of ten and the effect of excess powder on the conveyor was finally seen. Each conveyor cup jerked and rocked over the granules of powder like a car on a rocky road. Each transient event was faster than the eye could see without the aid of technology. The limits of human vision were integrating these small variations of conveyor cup movement into continuous motion.

The cause (powder) was not without effect in the packaging process. Each small bump increased the variation of package position when the package sealer fired. The excess powder materially increased the likelihood of a *registration* (position) error when the product was packaged and the position variability was the ultimate cause of scrapped product.

Sometimes the limitations of perception are not in the nature of our eyes and ears but in our willingness to use them.

A client was experiencing a small percentage of defects in its rubber glove manufacture. Hundreds of forms were pulled by conveyor through a hundred yards of machinery where they were washed, dipped in latex, then heated in a gas-fired oven.

Since the BTU (heat capacity) of natural gas can vary, operators knew they had to monitor the gas flows and occasionally adjust them to maintain a target temperature. "What does the gauge say?" I asked the operator.

"180." he said, knowing what the answer was -supposed- to be. He looked again. "160? 150?" He peered at the gauge through thick glasses.

Although there was plenty of cable length connecting the dial to the oven, maintenance had placed the temperature gauge at a height of 7 1/2 feet - well over the operator's head. Perhaps the last operator had been very tall!

This was not a failure of the near-sighted operator, but of the company. They did not value and facilitate attention to details.

The company's attitude to details and housekeeping was confirmed as I walked the long aisles between the machines. "What is this?" I asked.

"Why, it's just a small puddle of water. It's no big deal. Every one of these machines has an internal *washing* station where the latex forms are cleaned. Surely you can't blame a puddle of water in the aisle for scrap product! I just can't see any connection."

"We are looking for evidence of things that you *can't* always see." I said. "If the water is here, where is it *supposed* to be? What is behind that door?"

The door was an access panel to the washing station. It had not been opened in a while, and we moved it with difficulty. When we looked inside, a spray-washer was misaligned - pointed at the cabinet housing and not at the latex forms.

Because operators tend to forget or discount the unseen world beneath the threshold of perception, they don't always grasp the importance of housekeeping and attention to small details.

For example, one operator may neglect to use required gloves or wash their hands before handling a product. Or, they may imagine that they have a *technician's prerogative* and rearrange or even leave out steps in a critical process because *they can't **see** any difference!*

In order to progress past a certain point, business must educate their associates that a world exists outside their threshold of perception. Sometimes that world of details is revealed simply by opening a door.

11: How To Use A Dictionary

Words and concepts are not the same. Dictionaries quickly demonstrate this fact. Notice that the dictionary is a cross-reference between alphabetically organized words and ideas. Most words are followed by numbered entries, and each entry defines a different and particular idea.

The phrase, sentence, and paragraph surrounding a word establish a *context*, or framework, from which you can judge meaning. In good writing, context clearly directs you to a single meaning for every word, unless the author is trying to be clever.

Beware equivocation! Don't confuse yourself and others by vaguely blending the distinct meanings. In a written sentence or in speech, *"Parakeets"* might refer to either (a) small brightly colored tropical birds, or (b) *two* keets, but not both of these things! *Always Choose Just One Meaning*, and do it *before* you speak. Don't baffle or deceive your audience by your indecision.

Do read and think about the multiple meanings a word represents. Consider that the word ***root*** is sometimes used to refer to that part of a plant that sustains and anchors it, but the ***root*** of a problem is that fundamental idea or thing upon which the problem depends. If you know that a plant dies when its root is destroyed, then you more clearly understand why a speaker might urge you to attack "the *root* of a problem".

50

What Are The Odds you Can Use At Least One?

Use Synonyms! If you examine dictionary definitions of a word and don't find the exact shade of meaning you need – then look up similar words. It is, however, a reasonable last resort to use a word in a way that dictionaries do not document.

If you must use a word in an unconventional way, *you should also* provide at least a short acceptable definition. You might say: "Attack the *root* of the problem." Then, for clarity you could add: "By *root*, I mean that fundamental idea or thing upon which the problem depends."

This *hair-splitting* concern for meaning was actually a life-changing gift from my mother. I was seven years old or so, and just in from a day at school.

I must have shocked her with something new in my vocabulary because she said: "Don't you *ever* use a word again without knowing what it means!"

I don't know if my mother realizes the power and reach of that early life advice, but she has kindly forgotten the colorful word in my vocabulary that started it all.

12: Rational Team Building

Re-Organization and *Teams* are the perennials in the Management Improvement garden. Popping their heads above ground every weak financial spring, hope springs eternal for these two old favorites. While these venerable strategies do occasionally work to rejuvenate an organization, it isn't magic. *Understanding* that fact is the key to more than an occasional success.

With teams, the intent is to bring people together and charge them with a common purpose in the hope that they will *somehow* be more productive than individuals. For true believers, the *somehow* is guaranteed by faith and philosophy, but there are those of us who have seen teams perform *worse* than the proverbial "one good engineer".

Teams can be rationally formed or they can be mal-formed. They can be too big, be organized badly, or composed of the *wrong* people. Just as competent individuals are the building blocks of successful teams, properly formed teams are the building blocks of larger organizational structures. (In this strict use of the word, thirty people cannot form a team.)

In this article, we will focus on the issue of staffing a team. In another time and place we can discuss in more detail why teams need to be small (*No more than **six** individuals*), why the team leader is expected to be a working member of the team, and why the team leader is not the same as a supervisor, manager or coach. (A supervisor may be responsible for 2-4 teams.)

Teams have intrinsic *in*efficiencies. Team members need to communicate and to closely coordinate their actions. As a consequence, team communication and team meetings are often considered a boring, time consuming and necessary evil. The larger the team, the more these *overhead* costs sap productivity.

Teams can *still* be outstanding producers despite this innate disadvantage. They just need to be formed in such a way that they exploit one of several established principles of productivity.

1. **Division of Labor.** It has been known for generations that cooperating specialists can be more productive than generalists, *if* there is sufficient work to keep the specialty occupied. If there is not sufficient work, then the specialty work is absorbed into the closest skill match.

   You can take advantage of this principle by staffing a team with *__different backgrounds and skills__*. A team with a diversity of skills can maximize productivity if there is sufficient work to justify each specialty.

2. **Many hands make light work.** There are many jobs that are unpleasant, tedious and boring. Nevertheless, they must be done. A single good trooper who is assigned to *swamp draining* duties may intellectually appreciate that every job is important, but a long dreary task can sap the morale and productivity of the best.

   This kind of assignment generally calls for *__similar backgrounds and skills__*. A friendly peer is the best kind of team member to have by one's side when there is an undesirable assignment to be slogged through.

3. **Perspectives Generate Ideas.** Once again, here is a reason to staff a team with individuals selected for their *different backgrounds and skills*. There are times when we are *idea poor* and are looking for a fresh approach to a market, to a new product or for a problem solution.

   Teams of like mind tend to hash over the same old talking points and repeatedly converge on the same solution. Worse, as a result, they may deem their conclusion the best alternative because they do not have the benefit of a radically different perspective.

4. **Safety in Numbers.** A Team can be more productive than individuals if teams are formed as a *risk reduction strategy*. Think of this as adding a *Co-Pilot* or a *spotter* in any task where a single misstep or sudden loss of a key individual can be catastrophic.

   Similar *backgrounds and skills* would be characteristic of this kind of team. Here the advantage is intangible and a manager would need a good quantitative understanding of risk in order to fully appreciate what is bought by adding redundant team members.

What is the conclusion? Don't expect a team to be *somehow* more effective or motivated than the enthusiastic and committed individual. Form teams *for a reason*. Have an idea as to how a team might be more productive in *a given situation*. Then, staff the team accordingly, with individuals selected for either their common or complementary abilities. If you *can't* make a case for a team, then don't forget the effectiveness of "one good engineer".

13: SPC Caveat

I can't tell you the number of times that I have taken the Executive Facility Tour only to see something disappointing offered as their **S**tatistical **P**rocess **C**ontrol!

It's a control chart, demanding attention, loudly proclaiming that the process is *out of control*. However, the machinery still turns and product continues to be packaged and shipped.

Many of these operations have an abundance of quality certification banners. They have subscribed to the latest fashions in quality (e.g. Six Sigma, Total Quality, etc.). They have hired quality and engineering professionals who are expected to manage quality.

So, how can this be? How can an organization that values quality continue *business as usual* in the face of an urgent alert like this?

DISCOUNTED INFORMATION

In situations like these, the message conveyed by the control chart has been almost totally discounted. Its perceived relevance to decision-making is almost nil.

There was once a time when the TV weather report received the same scornful treatment. The report would recommend umbrellas and the sun would shine. People would smile and say, "I told you that you can't trust the weatherman!"

We all have noticed those new car indicators that suddenly urge you to take out your wallet and drive quickly to the nearest dealer/service center. "Check Engine", the message says, and from the vague discussion in the owner's manual - a folklore has sprung up.

"It's a computer malfunction." people say. "It's on a timer. It's connected to the odometer." others theorize. Ultimately, the information is *discounted, and* many people ignore the check engine warning.

Now, think about the *ignored control chart*. Like an unreliable weather report or a mystery auto *idiot light*, people have persuaded themselves that the information in the chart has *no relevance* to hour by hour workplace decisions.

There are three things which would cause SPC charts to be discounted and ignored.

1) Operations Not Properly Trained in SPC Based Decision-Making

Why wouldn't anyone in a room full of people answer a ringing phone? Perhaps everyone assumes the call is for *someone else*!

Control charts facilitate decision-making, but whose decisions? (**Operations!**) Too often, operations personnel assume the chart is for the quality folks , or for engineering or maintenance.

The first cause of control chart apathy is simply that operations personnel have been trained from a quality or engineering perspective, and have never been shown how they are utilized to make operational decisions.

2) Operations Leadership Encourages Process Short-Cuts

There are many operations managers and supervisors who do not place emphasis on doing a job right. *Right* to them is "whatever gets the alligator off your back". SPC may be screaming warnings but the folks who approve paychecks pay operators to ignore it.

3) SPC Really is Broken!

If you have a car with capricious warning indicators, you learn quickly to not take them seriously. If the various warnings appeared and disappeared for no apparent reason and careful observation of the car showed no problem, then the dashboard feedback is now dismissed as broken and worthless.

SPC control charts can be *broken*. There may be a minor or major technical flaw in the way data is gathered and presented, and this is the third cause of chart apathy.

COULD THINGS BE ANY WORSE?

The only thing worse than chart apathy is chart apathy with a veneer of correctness. A common mistake in response to these problems is a management directive to *make SPC look right*.

Charts are tweaked to look like the perfect case of *in control* - a mathematical version of telling the boss what he wants to hear.

HOW TO FIX THIS MESS

Operations, quality and engineering have different uses for SPC data. Start retraining and reimplementation with operations. The SPC-based decisions that engineers and quality personnel make depend on and assume a correct implementation of operations SPC.

To fix control chart apathy,

1) Start with a definition of a correct process. Managers and supervisors must reward work done correctly.

2) Rename control charts *Consistency Charts*. (That is what they really are!) Operations personnel need to understand what the chart is telling them about their work – that products being made now are inconsistent and measurably different than those that were made previously.

3) Control charts must be implemented in such a way that out-of-control indicators really are relevant to operations decisions.

   When change occurs, the organization must have a means to evaluate the product to determine if the change has produced improvement or deterioration. The cause of the change should be investigated, added to the inventory of process knowledge and (if possible) managed.

14: Procedure Or Process?

When I talk to clients about business processes and the importance of process knowledge, they often confuse *Process* with *Procedure*. The mistake is understandable. Both are *intentional methods* of doing business, and procedures are a far more common and familiar territory than process.

The reason that procedures are more common is most likely cost and skill. Procedure-building is similar to On The Job Training). A worker is designated best. An observer then documents behavior, and a technical writer prepares a procedure document that instructs others how to copy the example.

On the other hand, process-building is an engineering activity. It begins by considering the objective, and then the means to achieve it. Using scientific principles, available and potential tools, and considering alternatives, costs and quality, a correct method that reflects cause-effect is outlined, tested and implemented.

It is possible and likely that no worker presently meets the desired standard of performance before a correct process is created. This is why approaches that start by analyzing and diagramming *what we do now* are far inferior to a true process approach that begins by asking, "What result do we want, and on what activities does this depend?"

Procedures aim to preserve the status-quo by copying *something that works*. Processes aim higher.

PROCEDURES

Procedures are activity oriented. Step-by-step, they tell people what to do with little attention to why. In effect, procedures say, "Trust Me." and the good operator obeys.

In manufacturing, it is common to use procedure sheets, or manufacturing *recipes*. Years ago, I helped a client who made cast aluminum parts. The business had thousands of recipes specifying: mold #, fill pressures and fill times, and holding times for cooling.

Step-by-step, the operators faithfully followed these recipes, and year-by-year the parts yield gradually grew worse. The thermal and mechanical characteristics of the aluminum casting facility gradually changed over time. With age, maintenance, and repair - it was literally no longer the same machine.

Every year, an increasing number of the recipes were wrong, and the obedient operator had little choice but to run the procedure, and discover by trial and error which procedures were still valid.

PROCESSES

A **Process** approach made it possible to involve the operator's judgment, and to account for the change in the machine over time. *The good operator is one that thinks!*

By developing methods based on cause-effect relationships and process knowledge, we made it possible for operators to spot errors in recipes before the aluminum casting shot was fired!

*Thirty Seven Ideas For Business Operation Improvement**

Within a work-center, a business process is an intentionally designed baseline plan for roles, stations, tasks and targets. It is the organized knowledge of who does what, where, when.

Periodic measurements tell operations if the process is behaving according to its baseline, or if something has changed.

Knowledge of the anatomy, the cause-effect relationships in the process enables operations to understand and interpret measurements and variance, and to determine a corrective action.

NEED AN EXAMPLE?

A simple example is often helpful in separating and clarifying two similar ideas. The perfect case came to my mind as I deciphered the workings of our new digital camera.

The Procedure approach was useful for a quick start: 1) Turn The Power on. 2) Set Program Dial to P 3) Look At your subject through the viewfinder. 4) Press the Silver button.

This procedure helped me to take my first picture, but does not make me a photographer. For over one hundred years, the science of photography has been based on concepts of light, lens, focal point and image plane.

The process of photography begins with an understanding of the objective: a captured image where we control the illumination, color and contrast, depth of field, and motion. The key process metrics have always been: light sensitivity, grain (now, mega-pixels), aperture, exposure time and filtration.

What Are The Odds you Can Use At Least One?

From the Brownie box camera to the latest multi-mega-pixel digital, the science and basic process of photography has been remarkably stable, even though the procedures vary with camera model and circumstance.

The professional photographer uses this knowledge and current observable facts and measurements. By observing the lighting conditions, the degree of motion, colors and contrasts in the subject and the background, etc., it is possible to adapt to a changing environment and still produce excellent pictures.

Process Knowledge is so obviously the distinguishing characteristic of the professional photographer with a competitive advantage. Anyone else is a guy with a camera.

CONCLUSION

In a modern business, it is unacceptable to have gauges, controls, computer reports metrics, and machine adjustments which are mysterious unknowns to an operations work force that just follows recipes. The result is a slow creeping loss of competitiveness that many may not grasp until it is too late.

This condition is avoided by retaining, organizing and communicating process knowledge. The result is an operations capability that is consistent and robust even while things change.

Learn the tactical management skill of mastering the tools you have. If you can't run the existing facility correctly and consistently, capital expenditures on new toys are likely to let you make more expensive scrap faster!

15: The Iron Triangle

The consideration of the value or worth of a project objective always takes into account three dimensions:

Performance - *What is the deliverable?*

Timeliness - *When will the project be complete?*

Cost - *What is the total cost, including any hidden costs, of the project? (All costs ultimately reduce to effort.)*

The *Performance* dimension to a project objective describes the deliverable which is the target *and* tolerances (i.e. quality) of what will be produced or changed.

Working backwards, it makes sense that to *have* a desired result (e.g. piano skills) one must *do* certain things. (Practice!) Deliverables and a project strategy determine what *action*s, or *tasks,* must be accomplished in order to complete the objective.

When we analyze any *single* task that is *performed correctly,* we find something obvious: *It usually takes as long as it takes* and *costs what it costs.*

From these two facts, many people wrongly deduce that deliverables determine the time frame and the total cost in addition to the necessary and sufficient project tasks.

By this line of thinking, there is only **one** *independent* dimension to a project objective; the other dimensions cannot freely vary. Most project management texts *correctly disagree* with this conclusion.

MULTIPLE OUTCOMES FOR TIME AND COST

Projects are composed of *multiple concurrent tasks*. Because of this, *many* trade-offs between project completion times and costs are possible.

One trade-off is to extend the deadline. Extending the time line creates opportunities for efficiency. The astute manager seizes these opportunities and reduces costs. The alternative is to push for an early completion by paying expediting fees, overtime, etc.

Unfortunately, this has been oversimplified to the slogan, "You can have two of the three", meaning that Performance, Time & Cost form an unyielding Iron Triangle with only *two* independent dimensions. Additional deliverables must always be paid for by a later delivery time or by an increased cost.

This *Iron Triangle* view of the three dimensions to project objectives is only true in the simplest of projects, and it is often used as an excuse for poor project management.

There are at least three reasons **not** to subscribe to the *Iron Triangle* view of performance-time-cost.

BEATING THE IRON TRIANGLE

First, consider that it is *always* possible to spend *more* time and more money on any project without obtaining the *slightest improvement* in deliverables!

This thought should at least prepare you to consider the notion that deliverables may often be achieved with *less* time and money.

This achievement requires *active management*! It is a fact of life that the project environment will change. The fundamental tactical skill is the ability to detect significant change and to appropriately redeploy resources.

Estimating handbooks and estimates based on *comparables* will inevitably crank a bit of cushion into the costs, as they are based on averages. It is the standard deviation in these statistics that active management will exploit.

Good project management requires that the essential management tools be used. Task Plans, Resource Loading Analysis, good purchasing and accounts payable skills, critical path calculations and project tracking skills all facilitate the best use of time and money to achieve a deliverable.

If the project manager is not maintaining the kind of continuous focus necessary to obtain optimum results, then anyone who does maintain the required focus will certainly achieve a more desirable blend of performance-time-cost.

Second, the *trade off* of Performance-Time-Cost is extremely sensitive to project strategy.

What Are The Odds you Can Use At Least One?

Imagine a project where the first sub-objective is: ***Bring up an empty web site, ready for content.***

I could: a) Buy hardware ($2000), b) connect to the INTERNET ($90/month), c) load software (8 hours @ $50/hour).

Or, for less than a few hundred dollars, and 30 minutes of time, I could bring up the empty web site on a commercial service. They may even include perks like: backup services, maintenance, redundant connections to the INTERNET, backup power sources for high reliability and physical security services.

Of course, project strategy is not entirely in the control of the project manager. Authority for a choice of strategy flows from the customer. Most often, in complex technical projects, a project architect or program manager will speak on behalf of the customer with regard to strategic choices.

Still, project strategy is at least *partially* within the realm of the project manager's authority. Because of this, the *Iron Triangle* concept applies **only** in the unlikely context where every tactical advantage has been seized, when there are no strategic decisions left on the table *and when all the possibilities of a third factor have been exhausted!*

The Third Factor. There is *another* dimension in the equation for project value. The basic formula based on performance, time and cost essentially asks: 1) What are we going to get? 2) When will we get it? 3) What will it cost?

There is a fourth dimension and it is **Risk**.

Thirty Seven Ideas For Business Operation Improvement*

In the 1960s, when computer technology was new, it used to be said that "no one was ever fired for buying IBM". The company was the undisputed giant in automation. Customers often paid a heavy premium for products and services from what consensus said was a low risk vendor. (Today, people pay that *safety* premium to Microsoft.)

In the days when IBM dominated the computer market, only *maverick* managers bought products from smaller companies that were perceived to be *riskier*. When they succeeded, their projects beat the *Iron Triangle* of conventional wisdom.

Do not rush straightaway to the bargain shop just yet. In large numbers, *risk is real*. Unmanaged, the incorporation of products and vendors of lesser and unknown reputation can have unpredictable results. They will raise costs in one case while costs are lowered in another.

This secret to getting more in less time for less money lies in your ability to *manage* risk.

The two fundamental issues here are:

1. Where in the project does one use the so-called *high risk* vendor?

2. When a high-risk vendor or product is considered, can we identify the exact nature of the risk and mitigate it?

CONCLUSION

The most stubborn defenders of the Iron Triangle philosophy are often risk-averse project managers who always buy IBM, but every project of any size has a risk dimension that must be managed.

The essence of risk is uncertainty. A project manager is always asking, "Am I certain? How do I know?" These questions cannot be avoided by only choosing vendors and brands that are perceived as *safe*.

The project manager that actively redeploys resources as things change, exercises the available options for project strategy, and embraces the management of risk will *beat the Iron Triangle*.

16: Back To Baselines

Information that *cannot be readily accessed* when and where we need it *will not help* our decision-making. Fortunately, knowledge can be organized, condensed, and made *user friendly* by a number of techniques.

One powerful approach, particularly in the world of complex, technology-based business processes, is the organization of information as *Baseline & Change*.

EVERYDAY EXAMPLES

There are countless common examples that illustrate the principle. Here are just a few:

- An Electro-Cardiogram. Doctors recommend that people have one made when they are young and healthy!

  This earlier measurement serves as a *baseline* against which later tests can be interpreted in terms of any *change*.

- MPEG/Digital Video. You may have noticed that *tuning* in a television channel via digital cable or satellite may take a couple of seconds before sound and picture appears.

  This is because digital video is stored as a series of infrequent *baseline* images followed by just the information about *changes* to the picture!

- An old-fashioned dial combination lock. You can't just start dialing in the combination. You first have to restore the tumblers to a starting, or *baseline*, configuration.

  This is usually done by at least three complete turns of the dial in a particular direction. The proper turns to the right and to the left *changes* the tumblers in a consistent fashion from the *baseline* configuration.

- Experienced hikers avoid being seriously lost in the woods by consciously identifying *baselines*. They may, for example, note:

  - A stream runs throughout the middle of the area they wish to walk.

  - A road bounds the west side of the area.

  - A cleared area and a subdivision bounds the east.

  They are then free to explore within the limits of *baselines*. ("*I am between the stream and the subdivision.*")

- Real Estate appraisers use special baselines known as *comparables*. A *comparables analysis* begins by choosing two or three particular pieces of property with value established by recent sale.

  From this *baseline*, the appraiser adds or subtracts *changes* to the value of the property being valuated.

(e.g. "*A third bathroom adds $6000. to the appraised value, since the baseline, or comparable property, price was based on only two.*")

- When you misplace your car keys, you use the *baseline* concept! ("I know I had them when I left the office! What have I done *since then?*")

IF IT'S SO OBVIOUS....

Baselines are perfect tools for managing process knowledge in: computer network configurations, paint or printing color matching, chemistry components of manufacturing (plating solutions, latex tanks, chemical baths, etc.), precision machining setup, and more.

If this is such an obvious and powerful tool, why isn't it used more often and more effectively to improve productivity and quality in operations?

In operations audits, I often find:

- No two Infrastructure routers, hubs or spares configured the same way.

- Quality Assurance technicians puzzling over chemical tanks, grasping for analytical techniques that will *somehow* provide certainty about the contents. ("*What do you suppose is **in** there?*")

- Trial and error manufacturing setups. There may be one individual who can complete the job in a predictable amount of time, but can never seem to pass the skill along to anyone else.

WHAT'S HOLDING YOU BACK?

Obvious Does Not Mean Automatic. Just because a certain way of organizing information is obvious does not mean that it is automatic. There is a considerable amount of work just collecting and collating the various pieces of data required to begin to identify and establish an operations baseline.

Lack of Tools. The key benefit of a *Baseline & Change* method is the decisiveness that follows from being able to return to a known and predictable configuration or state. But there is generally a lack of familiarity with tools that allow you to describe a baseline and confirm when you have reached it.

Lack of Experience. Using a baseline is a different skill from identifying and establishing baselines. An experienced hiker who has been trained to use the baseline concept in the woods is not ready to automatically apply that experience to real estate appraisal.

Anyone can be instructed in how to use the *Baseline & Change* method in their particular field, but the ability to establish new uses is an uncommon engineering skill.

17: Category, Type & Item

Most people have called a support or *Help Desk* and they know that the better ones make a record of each customer contact in a ticketing system.

Help Desk tickets are more than automated *"called while you were out"* systems. Resting on top of reliable ticketing software is the ticketing *design*.

Service work by nature has many intangible qualities. A good ticketing design is what makes the efforts of a service operation visible, measurable and manageable.

An organization can purchase standard ticketing software on the basis of reliability, scalability, robustness, support and price. The ticket *design*, however, needs to be created in coordination with the operational design for the business and modified when the business changes.

The heart of the ticket design is often called **C**ategory, **T**ype and **I**tem classification. Tickets are classified for many reasons, including: accountability, service assignment and ticket routing, and metrics.

Well designed CTI systems allow a service tech to classify a ticket into one of a thousand categories by picking one of ten *categories*, then one of ten *types* and one of ten *items*.

Of course, this makes so much more sense than searching through a master list of dozens, hundreds (or more) of request types. However, this is not the most important aspect of a well designed CTI!

CTI PROBLEMS

Poor CTI coding can undermine metrics. When you look at tickets from badly designed classification systems, you will typically see a conceptually unusable hodgepodge of symptoms, diagnosis, prescribed solutions, prognosis and follow-up.

Good CTI ticket design is difficult. Perspectives on ticket classification change throughout its life cycle. What starts as a call for email assistance actually becomes an antivirus issue. Agents all too often will second guess themselves, or make too much use of the Other/Miscellaneous or User Error buckets.

CTI SOLUTIONS

I typically recommend that prior to creation of a CTI design, the organization make a dependency diagram of the *anatomy* of the technology they intend to support.

In a medical emergency room, a receiving nurse requires knowledge of patient anatomy before they can make *any* classification of a particular case. In a help desk, a similar kind of knowledge is required.

A dependency diagram highlights *causal* relationships and clearly shows *what depends on what*. From the dependency diagram, Categories are more easily created and then refined into Type and Item.

In a manner similar to the emergency receiving room, Help Desk agents should be trained think in terms of *symptoms* when they categorize a request as a Category, Type and Item.

CTI cannot be used to record both symptoms *and a diagnosis.*

HELP DESK WORK FLOW

I design ticketing systems around a work flow that *begins* with CTI and symptoms. Once established, the CTI is rarely touched. The second step in the work flow requires the collection of information and diagnosis of a likely *cause.*

The third and fourth steps also sound somewhat *medicinal.* I want Help Desk agents to *prescribe* a solution and close the ticket with a *prognosis* and if possible, an actual outcome.

All of this information cannot be stuffed into CTI fields. Many operations try. They get information about how the request was presented all muddled with actions taken, actual causes and outcomes. A good ticket design does not place all of these requirements on the CTI.

CONCLUSION

A properly organized CTI classification system should reflect the anatomy of the technology supported. It should recognize that, at first contact, there is only enough information for the pertinent *symptoms* and little more. Except for typing errors, CTI information should not be changed throughout the life of the ticket.

Additional fields on the ticket should collect information about likely causes, actions taken and outcomes *as the ticket is worked*. This information, together with the initial CTI of the ticket, creates a valuable *matrix* of information that will help operations improve and, in some cases, *eliminate* calls to the Help Desk.

18: What Is Decision Support?

Decision Support is the business function specifically charged with the question, *"What do we know about our operation, and how do we know it?"* Because of the difficulties in extracting information (*ideas*) from data, the ideal of Decision Support is difficult to achieve.

There are two essential activities that cause a *complete, clear and accurate picture* of the current state of the business to emerge: conceptualization and validation.

Conceptualization directs the grouping and summarization of data and the order and form of presentation. Validation presides over the integrity of the entire chain of facts, from measurement validation through data collection and statistical analysis to final presentation.

CONCEPTUALIZATION

In a business of any size, an idea of the current state of the business is typically presented as a collection of summaries. Endless pages of numbers, statistics, ratios, pie and bar charts do *not* have the decision-making impact of concise exhibits that are presented in a proper order.

What many people do not realize is that the conceptual *buckets* used in summarization are the key determinant as to what *idea* will emerge in the final analysis! The calculations of accounting or the automated statistics *dashboard* programs are just the mechanisms that will grind out a foreshadowed conclusion.

For example, you might see reports that contrast: East versus West Coast sales, plant #1 versus plant #2 profitability, 2nd shift versus 3rd shift utilization and manufacturing lot #12 versus lot #13 quality.

Now, East versus West Coast may *not be a crucial or even useful distinction*, and that is the point! Identifying which distinctions *are* critical is the most important function of sound Decision Support.

If such distinctions were intrinsic, any honest person could simply *look* and determine how to organize data into information. But proper organization of data into information is work that requires knowledge and skill.

Honest and accurate data will send the organization marching off in *exactly the* **wrong direction** *if it is badly summarized.*

AN EXAMPLE OF IMPROPER CONCEPTUALIZATION

I know an engineering team that spent months working on *the wrong things* because of a report that said: "*Your ten packaging machines have an average scrap rate of 1%*".

This report led the engineers to ask themselves, "*What do these ten machines have* **in common** *that would cause them to vary in their performance and occasionally produce scrap?*"

Expensive re-engineering proposals were thought to be the answer. AC motors would be replaced with precision DC *stepper* motors. Plastic parts would be replaced with stainless steel. Simple analog controllers would be replaced with computers and custom software would be developed.

A fresh approach to the data caused a *different* idea to emerge. The new report said: *"Packing machines 1-9 have a 0% scrap rate. Machine #10 is running 10% scrap!"*

Now engineering was asking a new question and was pursuing a solution in the exact *opposite* direction, *"What is **Different** about Machine #10?"*

DECISION SUPPORT SKILL SET

Although every business associate responsible for information reporting should be aware of the pitfalls, it is not common to find engineers, programmers, bookkeepers, or even technical and accounting managers who have the breadth of experience and skill to properly conceptualize data.

The largest companies with the *worst* business intelligence are those who *delegate down* Decision Support responsibilities to these departmental *silos* or to software vendors. There sometimes seems to be an attitude that such details are *beneath* top management.

An aptitude for Decision Support is a quality of the generalist, a higher level manager who has a breadth of business knowledge and experience combined with sufficient technical depth to exercise oversight of the technicians and information systems that extract actionable ideas from data.

What Are The Odds you Can Use At Least One?

Decision Support oversees *Information Architecture* at the highest level, where actionable information emerges from the data. It focuses on the business ideas hidden within the data, and is not distracted by the numbers, calculations and graphs. It is key to accuracy and timeliness in decision-making.

19: Having One's Own Opinions...

is not the same as thinking for oneself.

20: Creating Jobs Is Easy - Creating Wealth Is Hard

To the politician, Business exists to provide jobs and pay taxes. But, as one economist noted, important jobs with life or death consequences (and presumably a correspondingly high employee self-esteem) could be created overnight by placing the unemployed in charge of busy intersections and turning off the automated traffic lights.

This easy change, if mandated, would create many jobs but would destroy wealth. "Broken Window" economics creates jobs in the short term, but what about tomorrow?

To the naive, Business exists to *get* money. By this poor standard, cat burglars, grifters and extortionists could meet the definition of businessman.

An immature child of a financially secure home might think in terms of how to get his share of the family pie, but the adult that characterizes "distribution of natural abundances" or "rationing of scarcities" as the fundamental economic issue is destructively wrong.

To the entrepreneur, Business is the only tool that can *create* **substantial** *new wealth*. It's somewhat obvious how machinists, welders, and even artists and writers create things of value – but *how* does the businessman do it? There are at least three ways and one is fundamental.

Thirty Seven Ideas For Business Operation Improvement*

INNOVATION

Businesses take long-term risks with capital, and *innovate*. If successful, they cause energy, materials and, most importantly, time to be used more effectively. Failing businesses waste everyone's time and money, and destroy wealth.

Successful innovators are always reformulating in order to extravagantly *waste* the least expensive and most abundant commodity and to recycle, conserve and spare the most precious. This has always been the nature of enterprise and has never needed the pious urgings and second-guessing of eco-worriers.

TAKING CARE OF BUSINESS

In addition to innovation, a successful business must "Milk the cow", or if you prefer: "Feed the goose and collect the golden eggs." More than one brilliant business innovation has been frittered away by corporate leaders who measured the importance of correct, consistent and capable operations by their own lack of interest.

Operations savvy is about more than just cutting costs. Looking for the proverbial one less olive per jar, nickel and dime-ing customers on fees, and squeezing employees, is a *parody* and a misdirection.

CONCEPTUAL INTEGRITY

There is a third fundamental factor in the creation of wealth. Conceptual Integrity is the degree to which we can use concepts to organize and think about our operations, our products and our customers.

The power to think "in principle" is the power to simplify. This allows us to more intensely focus on that which matters. CI *enables* innovation and lean operations through mental empowerment. It is how "ease of doing business" is measured.

Conceptual Integrity's opposite is Conceptual Fragmentation. Conceptual Fragmentation is an approach to the business that swings between two unhelpful extremes.

One day, it is a complex piecemeal, *"no two snowflakes are alike"* perspective of customers, products, and work. The next day, work is *over-simplified: "Every order is basically the same except for part numbers."* In both extremes, the few crucial distinctions one needs to think about are not identified.

Consider this illustration:

*A retail business that deals with **200** part numbers **simplifies** their operation by organizing those items as 10 sizes, 5 colors and 4 styles.*

By factoring into conceptual units like size, color, and style, we simplify and organize in a manner appropriate for a human being.

Thirty Seven Ideas For Business Operation Improvement*

We increase the Conceptual Integrity of the business by reducing all product permutations and combinations to a few simple and understandable factors like size, color and style.

FACTORING

Conceptual Integrity *increases* when an organizing *change makes it easier* to think in principle about the work, the customers, the products, the business identity, etc. We call this organizing and simplifying process: *Factoring*.

Just as a large number (e.g. 270) can be reduced to it factors (2's, 3's and 5's), many aspects of a business can be simplified by identification of the key conceptual factors. *But Be Warned!*

Mathematical factoring is one of the most difficult problems of Mathematics! Simplifying a business operation to a few conceptual fundamentals is a non-trivial task; a certain breadth of knowledge is a prerequisite.

In a factored and focused operation, there is a sense of *anatomy*, an understanding of what depends on what. The work is easier to perform. The products and services are easier to sell.

Conceptual Integrity is a creative cause of wealth. Conceptual Fragmentation destroys wealth, and will undermine the gains achieved through innovation and diligent operations.

21: Ease of Use

Technology products are often evaluated on their *ease of use*. More important is the degree to which a customer finds your **company** easy or hard to do business with.

I just installed a DSL modem for a friend. It was extremely frustrating to have what should have been a ten minute process turn into more than an hour.

The ISP had wrapped the install process inside a *"the installer must be using one the following versions of Windows"* installation program.

This software installation wizard not only harvests an excessive amount of personal data, it up-sells, intrusively surveys, explains in too much detail how to put a modular plug in a jack, changes home pages in browsers and dumps dubious utility programs to the hard drive.

The company had turned what should be a very simple process into a tedious, pedantic waste of time. Such practices may survey well with novices and poorly with experts, but do not misinterpret these results.

The novices know of no alternative. If they successfully finish their self-install before they get hungry or before nature calls, they will write this off to the complex nature of technology and not to a poor business practice.

Thirty Seven Ideas For Business Operation Improvement*

I don't want to exhaust your attention with too many *difficult-do-to-business* stories, but here are a few *true story* teasers to broaden the scope:

- Businesses that claim their accounting systems cannot generate an invoice until AFTER you pay.

- Equipment model numbers that make no rational sense, and are designed to obscure true product differences and product obsolescence. (Be honest folks. It's *Last Year's* Model!!)

- Tedious authentication and security practices that are easily subverted, but are perfunctory hurdles that honest customers must jump just to get even a simple answer to a FAQ from customer support.

- Voluminous contracts for small purchases that hide important considerations in a sea of words that recapitulate the obvious, the usual and the customary. (Like the previous sentence!)

- Incessant meaningless customer surveys from companies who have no obvious mechanism to submit complaints and unsolicited feedback. (Tell us how *good* we are doing.)

...and more.

Aside from those who would misrepresent under the cover of legal cleverness, there are two obvious drivers that cause ease of doing business to trend in the wrong direction.

What Are The Odds you Can Use At Least One?

First, in an effort to cut costs, companies sometimes make life harder for customers. They *transfer* costs to the customers by requiring them to spend increased time following company processes or simply waiting in queue for services.

Difficulties in doing business are a hidden cost, and new customers do not take this into account when they judge a product's price and value.

These *transferred costs* do not have the sticker shock of a price increase, but money is time and hidden costs do not remain hidden. Buyers eventually realize, "*If I had known then what I know now about company X, I would have done without their product.*"

Second, and more fundamentally, there is a rampant misunderstanding of *Business Process*. I'll put the truth as clearly as possible. Business Process is what your *company* does, not what your customer must do.

If your business processes are right, customers will find buying from your company as easy as buying from a vending machine. "*Make your selection. Put your money in. Take the product. Enjoy!*"

Good process architecture makes this miracle happen and a customer need not know or care what goes on behind the *employee* entrance.

Note that I did *not* say, that "customers should not know" about business processes, only that they *need* not know. The degree to which business processes should be transparent varies by industry and has legal implications as well as policy and strategy considerations.

22: The Rest Of The Story...Frame of Reference

A few years ago, I did some consulting and training for a manufacturing company. Components of their products were made from metal castings with some precision requirements below a thousandth of an inch. The company had some trouble achieving these tough product targets and I was there to help.

Now put yourself in the management of this operation as you read, and ask yourself, *"What would I do?"*

BLUEPRINTS

All of the metal components were machined according to mechanical drawings (blueprints). After some research into the prints I made an interesting discovery. Many of the prints had a common flaw.

Let me simplify the story here to help you make a mental picture. Imagine that a hole is to be drilled into an eight inch wide block and the blueprint calls for the hole's center to be exactly four inches from the left edge and five inches from the right.

Now, make the mental picture. *Do the math!* See the problem? The drawing is ambiguous! There are two possible places that the hole could be formed.

Errors of this sort are avoided in drawings by measuring all dimensions from a single common *reference point or surface*. A single *frame of reference* means that everyone interprets blueprints and measurements in the same way.

The engineering drawings had many of these *multiple reference point* errors, and I brought this to the attention of management.

Now, if you were responsible for managing this company, **what would you do?**

PRESORT

I further researched the machining processes and found a long line of machining work centers. Each work center added one cut into a rough metal casting and finished parts were produced at the end of the line.

This *pipeline* approach had tremendous potential to rapidly turn out quantities of product. Like an assembly line, once the equipment was configured to make a certain kind of part, work *flowed* through the line and all of the machines stayed busy until an order was complete.

Everyone knew that the first machining work center was extremely critical. The first cut established a smooth flat *reference surface*. Every subsequent act of positioning, measuring or cutting began by lining up that flat reference surface in a standard position.

The problem was that the finished parts came off the line *significantly different*. Statistical analysis showed four distinct

91

groups which were traced back to a *casting mark* of **A**, **B**, **C**, or **D**.

The molds for the iron castings created four parts at a time. Parts that came from mold **A** were very much like any other **A**, but different from **B**. The difference was small, but enough to produce significant scrap.

I recommended that we add one work center to the start of the machining line. The job was simply to *sort* the castings by mold. Castings marked **A** would be processed and then the cutting machines would be re-calibrated before **B** parts would run.

We did an experiment. We tested the sorting station theory. Setup time was dramatically reduced because *first production piece* Quality inspections came back without delay. Every part now left the first machining work center with a consistent reference surface, and the finished parts came out at the end of the machining line as the *same* and not as *four flavors*.

Now, after this little experiment succeeded, if it were your facility and your money, **what would you do**?

THE EIGHT STATION TURNTABLE

Finally, there was a third story to tell from this same plant. It is a story that I have told in some detail in a previous article, but here is the abridged version.

A work center was designed as a round turntable. Seven stations with cutting tools were arranged around the table. The eighth station was a standing position for an operator to attach and remove parts from the table.

The operator would unload a finished part, load a fresh part, and then start the cycle. The table would rotate 45 degrees and each of the seven machining stations would go to work on their respective parts.

The machine had a terrible reputation with the operators and no one wanted to be responsible for setting it up for a customer order. After some investigation, I found out why.

The two stations on either side of the operator and the center of the table were designed to form a perfect 90 degree angle for reference and measurement. All placement of fixtures on the table and all positioning of the remaining five stations were to be made from this objective and absolute frame of reference.

I discovered that someone had unbolted and moved one of the two reference machining stations in an attempt to set up the machine. The perfect right angle was broken and a 89 or 91 degree angle had taken its place. It was now *impossible* to perform precision machining at this work center.

The only solution was to reposition the two critical stations relative to the center of the table. This required the machine manufacturer's assistance and the use of precision laser measurement tools.

So once again, if it were your responsibility, **what would you do**?

Here is the rest of the story.

Thirty Seven Ideas For Business Operation Improvement*

Regarding the blueprints:

The company decided to do nothing.

Regarding the new *presort* work center:

The company decided to do nothing.

Regarding the machine damaged by an untrained setup operator:

The company decided do nothing, and to leave the machine at it was.

The next time your engineers, plant managers, training or quality personnel tell you: *"we did SPC, measurement studies, process management, all those things...and they didn't make a difference in our scrap rate."* - take that with a big grain of salt, and get the rest of *their* story.

If you continue to do what you always did, you'll get what you always got.

23: What is a Fair Price?

Conceptual Integrity in operations is the degree to which we can use concepts to organize and think about our work, our products and our customers. The power to think *in principle* about our operations is the power to simplify our business and allows us to more intensely focus on that which matters.

CI is a *measure* of the degree to which we have made it easy to do business both as an associate and as a customer. (See Article #20: *Creating Jobs Is Easy.*)

RATIONALIZED PRICING

The idea of rationalized pricing is CI applied to product pricing. The customer wants to understand quickly and clearly: *"What do I get? What do I pay? What are the hidden costs? What is the value ratio?"*

The seller wants to avoid unintended incentives and "sweet spots" in the pricing that accidentally cause customers to buy the *three pack* instead of the *ten pack*.

Some businesses do not benefit from such clarity. However, all things equal, clarity in price facilitates *ease of doing business*. Within an industry, a straightforward rate strategy eventually will drive out the byzantine.

Cell phone services still have portions of the monthly statement that are quite inscrutable but for the most part the clarity of wireless service billing has consistently improved over two decades.

Thirty Seven Ideas For Business Operation Improvement*

In the early 1990's cellular customers had a mild panic attack each time the statement arrived. With variable per minute rates, and stiff roaming charges for just talking while *passing by* a competitor's cell tower, bills were seen as an unpredictable liability.

In the late 90's, "One Rate" plans effectively eliminated roaming rates and made it substantially easier for customers to anticipate their bill. Shortly after the first major carrier eliminated roaming, the entire industry found itself dragged into the new world of "One Rate" billing.

The subsequent trend was flat-rate unlimited plans for voice and also for data. *What could be simpler!*

Again, one carrier was first and others had no choice but to quickly follow. Twice in a decade and within the same industry, we see price simplification resulted in an irresistible competitive advantage.

THINGS CHANGE

Today (2011), with surging data usage over wired and wireless media, there is a bit of grumbling and *flat-rate remorse* from vendors. They talk of caps on usage, overage fees and even disconnecting "abusive" users.

Some of this is the result of the industry's short term *infrastructure* growing pains. I personally have doubts about longer term bandwidth scarcity. I don't think usage rationing will be the driving factor that causes companies to abandon the popular flat-rate and unlimited cellular service plans. *We'll see.*

Unfortunately, scarcity is the sales pitch that some companies today are using to try to sell their customers an alternative to the simple and straightforward unlimited service plans.

"Other customers are using more than their fair share." you may be told. But cookie-jar analogies will not be enough to persuade more than a guilt-ridden few that we *ought not* to want unlimited service plans.

Despite the current overwhelming popularity of flat rate pricing and the limited effectiveness of guilt in closing sales, I *can* see an emerging future trend where customers *will embrace* usage-based billing and change the industry!

THE FRUGAL MILLIONAIRE

Presently, wired customers pay a fixed price for unlimited use of a data pipe of a certain capacity. Faster Internet connections have a higher flat rate, and slower connections are less. It is hard to imagine any incentive for a typical customer to want to abandon such an arrangement. It seems fair and scalable.

Like *"all you can eat buffets"* there will be a natural distribution of *heavy and light eaters* of wired data services. This in no way precludes a successful business model and the determination of a reasonable and profitable flat-rate price.

Customers of buffets are legitimately prohibited from taking home hams in their pockets, and customers of wired data services cannot legally retail their network access to neighbors.

Imagine though, the *frugal* millionaire who has a dozen homes all wired with broadband. Flat rate contracts will provision each house with Internet services even though they may be occupied a month or less each year, but the value calculation becomes more complex.

> *"Shall I turn the service on and off as needed? Are there activation fees for that? Perhaps one home will be connected and the other left dark. Can I live with that?"*

To this hypothetical customer, *flat rate per house* services begin to look *burdensome and inflexible*. The company that offers simple, reasonably priced *usage-based service becomes a conceptually simpler and therefore more attractive alternative*.

> *"Transfer 50 gigabytes of data, pay for 50 gigabytes."*

To our frugal millionaire, what could be simpler? (Provided of course, that the cost of a gigabyte continues to trend down and the usage price is not seen as gouging.)

FUTURE OF THE WIRELESS INDUSTRY

The wireless data world is on the cusp of a major change. LTE networks are IPv6 *all data* networks with a potential of millions of unique IP addresses for each living person. Even telephone calls will eventually travel end-to-end across LTE as packets of data.

It is a world standard that will rapidly drive radio hardware prices to incredibly inexpensive levels. Instead of just one or two phones and an iPad, more and more homes will have *many* data-capable electronic devices.

Many next-generation gadgets will have an embedded cellular modem and an IP address whether you care, use it or not. We will *all* be like the hypothetical *frugal millionaire* with many infrequently used devices that benefit from connectivity.

When wireless data customers begin to add up the $15, $20 and $30 monthly unlimited usage fees on phones, tablets, digital cameras, and more, *pay for use* wireless data will then be seen as *the better idea.* It will be considered the simple, rational, flexible and *fair* way to price wireless data services.

Amazon's Kindle foreshadowed this change. Each Kindle shipped with an activated cellular data radio. There were no monthly fees and no activation fees – only usage fees.

This arrangement made ownership of a Kindle as a second or third data device a manageable and affordable cost. Data fees could even be bundled into the costs of other services such as eBooks and media.

The story of price in the wireless industry illustrates the contextual nature of Conceptual Integrity. When things fundamentally change, when *causes* change, we *re-factor.*

The ideas we use to organize, simplify and run our business need to be periodically revisited. What is a usual and customary policy across an industry can become inflexible and archaic in less than a decade.

24: The Extra Degree

I was inspired by the title and premise of a recent book. Since I haven't read the book yet, I hope the author will forgive me if I plough some of the same ground in this short article.

The book reminds us of the difference between boiling water and steam. With that one degree of difference, steam can move a locomotive. With images of the tiny difference between a prize winning race time and an Olympian "also ran" we are motivated to push for that extra effort that can *make a difference in degree into a difference in kind.*

Our mental life is a continual process of conceptually noting that things are either more or less the same or significantly different. *The Extra Degree* is a good reminder for us that there are transition points in context and our thinking where things can be *both.*

It is true that human and chimp intelligence has similarities that differ just in degree. This perspective lets us see our common primate nature in contrast with, say, chickens and fish. But, it is also true that there is a vast difference in kind that emerges somewhere between monkey and mankind. By a fundamental distinction, humans are a *uniquely different* kind of animal.

The business significance of "Degree and Kind" first appears in **Business 101**. The *Break-even* analysis looks at operations costs as the sum of fixed costs and additional variable costs which increase along with sales.

Few businesses can be profitable on one sale per year, and *break-even* is that point where the rate of sales breaks through to a difference in kind. It is that point where sales come in fast enough to pay variable costs and fixed costs with some profit remaining! Past the break-even point, profits begin to climb rapidly.

The tantalizing prospect of a breakout - to be ahead of the others in the race, to move past the break-even point and reap the reward of just a little more effort, is motivating to us all.

Another popular book confirms that **Outliers**, the virtuosos of their chosen profession, differ primarily from their peers in that they have *put in the time*. Experts in their field are found investing 10,000 hours to intensively master a subject or skill, emerging past this vocational sound barrier as an acclaimed leader.

There is a *companion strategy that makes hard work more effective:* **Move the boiling point.** Many do not know that under certain conditions, water can boil with just the heat from your hand!

Savvy businesses can move their break-even point from higher volumes in good times to lower volumes in recession. By restructuring the way they do business, they trade a higher fixed cost for lower variable costs and increase profitability at high sales volumes. The reverse maneuver is harder but often possible when sales trends weaken.

Strategies that *move the boiling point* are what some call *disruptive change* or *game changers*. We are fortunate to live in a time where opportunities to restructure our work and life abound, but in-house *continuous improvement* processes may miss many of these opportunities. Ideas are often constrained by legacy, precedent and status-quo that *pushes back* against even small evolutionary changes.

Entire industries often blind themselves to these kinds of possibilities by only hiring for leadership from *within* their industry. Newbies to the field are welcomed only in the first rungs of the ladder where they are left long enough to be thoroughly convinced that current practice is the only one and best.

We'll always be inspired by the prospect of *breakthrough*, and the success of champions and heroes. Such images help us to remember to keep on task, to keep focused, to try again, and to work a little harder.

But, along with this we should always be working *smarter*. We should always be on the lookout for ways to move that "Difference in Kind" a few degrees in our favor.

25: Troll Alert!

On the Internet, a TROLL is someone who baits an innocent into a war of words in a discussion forum. The object of the argument is not truth or knowledge, but a slice and dice victory at any cost. Trolls love to play this game for hours. (Google:"What is an Internet Troll?" in Wikipedia for more information.)

Now, I have heard Troll behavior called "sport", "spoiling for a fight", "jerking someone's chain", "gotcha", "bullying" and a couple of more vulgar expressions. Every time the innocent gives the troll the benefit of the doubt (*"Maybe they -really-want to know the answer to that question."*), the Troll gleefully says *"I can't believe they fell for it again!"*

Managers need to know that troll behavior does not occur only in cyberspace. Many times, those *core teams* whose meetings never end, are tricked into ploughing the same ground again and again by a troll in their midst. As a leader, you need to be able to spot and squelch a troll or they will destroy the morale and productivity of your team.

No weight of argument will forcibly write **Truth** on a human mind. One must press the mental "Total" key and **draw** a conclusion. Many people do not realize this, and Trolls exploit this naiveté.

Trolls delight in sowing and exploiting uncertainty in others and will either mirror that uncertainty or become a dogmatic and definite doubter as the game advances.

*Thirty Seven Ideas For Business Operation Improvement**

My advice? Master enough Parliamentary Procedure to *call the question* once evidence has been presented and debated. Learn to adjudicate. Learn to choose. Be willing to accept a few small mistakes. It is the price of leadership.

Oh, and one last thing: *Don't feed the trolls!*

26: What Can You Tell Me That I Don't Already Know?

I have had many skeptics arrive at my classes. Sent by their managers, some are convinced they know it all or at least *know enough.*

There are also those with low expectations who have previously endured the uninspired *copy of a copy* management training typical of large corporations. Others have much to *unlearn* from leadership by bad example.

These doubters may think but only rarely have the courage to ask, *"What can you tell me that I don't already know?"*

What people often *know* when they come to a training class is the syllabus - *the words* on the agenda. Many wrongly assume that terms like *efficiency, dependency* and *capability* refer to their everyday meanings, and they do not fully understand important technical and management concepts.

Even if students recognize that there is a new usage for an old familiar word, without study they are often unable to apply the concepts. Outside the classroom, one cannot put these ideas into practice by simply consulting the dictionary definitions.

If a subject is presented well and in the proper order, the material *flows.* It *does* seem obvious and familiar. When I am at my best, students could certainly leave one of my classes with a *"I think I already knew that – it was easy!"* feeling. For me, that is my measure of success. For the student, it is the beginning of the journey and not the end.

Mature knowledge is rich with inter-connections. It is organized as a dense network of relationships. More connections and **more insights are always possible**. The *deeper study* of a subject that you know brings maturity; it brings *wisdom* to your knowledge and enables you to know when and where to *apply* it.

27: Efficiency or Effectiveness?

Words and ideas are not the same. So, when two close conceptual cousins need consideration, we pause to define each term, and illustrate differences with examples.

Two important and closely related ideas are those of *efficiency* and *effectiveness*. Let´s establish our meaning for *efficiency* first, and then tackle the distinction that can mean success or failure in your operation.

EFFICIENCY

Miles per gallon is a good first example of the concept of *efficiency*. One car can travel 17 miles on one gallon of gas and another can travel 34. The second is said to be twice as efficient as the first and is able to travel a mile for the marginal cost of one nickel versus a dime.

Or consider a laborer who moves bricks a half dozen at a time in a five minute walk from the supply pallet to the working mason. A cart or a conveyor could allow this worker to move 100 times the material for a dollar of his time.

Efficiency describes activity per dollar. More activity per dollar is what brings a gleam to the eyes of accounting oriented managers, and of course, lowering unit costs is a positively wholesome thing.

However, in your business operation, efficiency is the *second* most important thing. An operation can be ruined if that which is *most* important is sacrificed in the name of efficiency. That *most* important consideration will be discussed towards the end of this article.

EFFICIENCY PITFALL #1

The *Efficiency Expert* is in fashion from time to time and it is a ripe subject for humor and parody. The quest for more motion per dollar frequently and predictably stumbles into classic error.

The first predictable error is *sub-optimization*. Efficiency gained in one task is lost by waste in another task. Is our bricklayer better off using the conveyor when we consider the time and cost required to set up and configure the conveyor? When all is said and done, exactly how many bricks are there to move?

The sub-optimization mistake is rampant in the world of computer technology. A fortune is typically spent in systems development and training for an infrequent task that could better be done by hand.

"The computer could do that" is a powerful and dangerous utterance in the wrong hands. This is one of the reasons why *customer driven* custom business software usually turns out to be such a disaster.

Without an architect who understands technology form and function, programmers take direction from end users, ad hoc steering committees and surveys of user wishes and needs.

The result is a sub-optimized mess, and workers learn to fear promises that "the computer will make your job easier."

Full optimization for efficiency is a difficult task. Consider the two vehicles that move at rates of 17 versus 34 miles per gallon. The efficiency equation suddenly looks very different if we realize that the low mileage vehicle seats eight passengers, while the gas sipper seats only two!

Finally, what about the *costs* of the two vehicles? If the eight seater costs a fortune, then opting to move eight people at a time may conserve gasoline and improve the P&L while damaging the balance sheet.

EFFICIENCY PITFALL #2

The second predictable error of the Efficiency Expert is the transfer of costs to another department or to the customer which *moves and hides* costs instead of reducing them.

Self Service strategies sometimes backfire for this reason. The cost savings anticipated by replacing live agents with automation is sometimes not realized because the solution is not engineered from the customer's point of view.

If a self-service solution is perceived by the customer as an unanticipated extra burden of effort and time imposed by the use of your product, then they may begin to question the *value-quotient*.

When they weigh what they get versus what they pay in transaction time and complexity, they may come to regret their decision to buy.

EFFICIENCY PITFALL #3

The third predictable error is the outright diminishing of value in the name of cost reduction. How many times can we play the "one less olive in the bottle" approach to cost reduction? How many times can we reduce the arm and legroom in a coach airline seat? Where is the point where the game is over?

We ask any manager with a mania for cost reduction to think about this and imagine that cost reduction carried to the ultimate and absurd extreme.

What are the values produced by a business that has *zero* costs? None! Zero Inputs = Zero Outputs! Businesses create value not by eliminating expenditures but by *spending well*.

EFFECTIVENESS

By *effectiveness,* I **do not** mean that obscure concept in manufacturing utilization calculations. I refer to *efficacy* - to *getting the job done*!

Effectiveness is the standard by which we judge money as well spent or wasted. Did it advance us toward the goal or was it a diversion? Did the purchase help us improve the value-quotient for the customer or was it irrelevant?

A sick man acutely in need of a hospital does not need *efficient public transportation*. If someone has a heart attack, they **do not** crawl down to the bus stop, wait twenty minutes and then change to the hospital express at the downtown station.

No! In a medical crisis someone calls 911, and we expect a big *inefficient* gas guzzling ambulance to promptly deliver the patient to the hospital.

Efficiency weighs *activity per dollar*, but is it the *right kind of activity?* Is it the kind of action that with every stroke creates value for the customer, or is it an action that, no matter how efficient, contributes nothing?

EFFICIENCY *AND* EFFECTIVENESS

Every successful business embraces *effectiveness* as the first virtue and *efficiency* as the important second.

As Peter Drucker said, *"There is nothing so useless as doing efficiently that which should not be done at all."* To make such determinations, one must have a standard of effectiveness, of value. This requires a strategic perspective, a grasp of corporate mission, goals, values and risk.

Real operations improvement *enhances effectiveness and improves efficiency,* but it must be directed from a strategic position where the Improvement Architect can see each initiative's impact on company policy, mission and vision.

28: Undercover Boss and the Red Zone

I recommend the TV show *Undercover Boss*, even though I rarely watch it. I *work* in the *Red Zone* and I don't need to see it every week on TV. Nevertheless, it is a *brilliant* television idea. It is absolutely vital that business leaders validate their notions of how their people work.

THE RED ZONE

The *Red Zone* is that gap between what management imagines and what actually happens. It is the gap between the IT department and its users, between engineers and operators, between training departments and customer-facing work-centers, between metrics and reality.

It is the neglected realm of strategy, business architecture and process engineering, neglected because everyone wrongly assumes that *someone else* is knowledgeable and responsible.

RED ZONE CAUSES

Secret Shoppers and Undercover Boss *job swapping* are clever ways to uncover dysfunctional Red Zones, but businesses are complex systems where every action has a reaction.

Red Zone gaps are often the result of adaptive behavior by well intentioned *Good Troopers*. Good Troopers are the ones who brag that when the boss says "*Jump!*", they say, "*How high?*".

If a tool is missing or a part doesn't fit, the Good Trooper takes it as a personal failing. "*If I needed a hammer, management would have provided it*", the Good Trooper says. They will try anything and everything to fix it *somehow*, unaware of the unintended consequences of their efforts.

BOSSES CAUSE RED ZONES TOO!

Somehow is a recipe for unintended consequences. Operators, supervisors, and tactical managers should be dealing almost exclusively with *how*, in a correct and consistent process. *Somehow* means that an operations Red Zone is forming.

Correctly transforming *somehow* into *how* is a management responsibility. A sequel to Undercover Boss might be titled "*How Hard Can it Be?*", since Red Zone problems can also begin by *management* failure to appreciate the importance of engineering clear methods for work.

The few Undercover Boss episodes that I have seen typically reveal who the *Good Troopers* are, and they are rewarded for their good intentions. Sadly, others are often chided and inspired to "*try harder*". It is rare when the Undercover Boss critiques methods, processes and tools and says something like: "*Why don't you have a hammer?*"

RED ZONES DO NOT EMPOWER

It is counter-intuitive, but clearly defined methods for work (exactly *how*, and not *somehow*) is an essential ingredient to empowering employees. Incentives and bonuses to the Good

Trooper who "figures it all out" is an abdication of a critical management activity.

Successful delegation requires independent thought. If we want our employees to be more than just obedient arms and legs while we *bottleneck* decision-making, then we must *set the table* by establishing strategically correct processes. Within this objective realm, associates can confidently make decisions that they will be able to defend as rational.

29: Willing And Able

There is no limit to what a productive man or woman is *able* to do.

There is no limit to what a destructive man or woman is *willing* to do.

30: Call Center Strategies

What is wrong with most call centers? The answer is: flawed strategy, flawed tactics and misuse of some very old mathematical models. If management is not focused on the proper essentials, the result is high costs and dissatisfied customers.

Wrong assumptions about what is important in call center operations leads to a *no-win* alternative. Either throw money at the problem or live with customer dissatisfaction.

ERLANG

One hundred years ago, a hands-on Danish mathematician climbed into Copenhagen manholes to study telephone traffic. Without knowing who called, why they called, what was discussed or any other particulars, he began to mathematically describe what he saw.

By mathematically modeling call arrival times, **Agner Krarup Erlang** found that average call volumes and durations could predict busy signals, line utilization and the number of rings until a circuit was connected. This, of course, applied to "calls in the wild" - anyone calling anyone for any reason or for no reason at all.

One interesting characteristic of *Erlang* calls is that call duration is heavily skewed to a shorter duration. Most calls are short, some are longer and a few calls straggle in with extraordinarily long call duration.

What Are The Odds you Can Use At Least One?

Citing Erlang, conventional call center wisdom makes two big mistakes.

MISTAKE NUMBER ONE

Call centers look for ways to create large pools of agents. This is a strategy for coping with variation driven by call arrival times.

This makes common sense in the cases where there are only a few agents and Erlang ("Erlang-C") calculations support this. A small team of agents will be able to take more calls and achieve higher utilizations than if they worked independently.

However, Erlang-C also predicts 90%-95% utilizations and short call hold times when call center sizes reach fifty to one hundred agents. This prediction rarely if ever holds true. *Do we really think call center problems go away when they grow to employ more than fifty agents?*

The advantages of agent pools diminish rapidly when they increase above the size of a small team. Something else begins to influence productivity!

MISTAKE NUMBER TWO

Since popular workforce management packages have only Erlang call durations built into their assumptions, and since most telephone systems are built to encourage large agent pools, tactical managers are taught to *fight* rather than properly *manage* other sources of variation.

Thirty Seven Ideas For Business Operation Improvement*

In the well-intentioned (but wrong) schools of call center management, supervisors are taught two things:

Force Agents to answer the phone as quickly as possible.
Force Agents to hang up the phone as quickly as possible.

WHAT CALL CENTERS CAN MANAGE

Processing time is a signature metric of a correct and consistent process.

A medium rare steak takes a predictable number of minutes to cook (plus or minus). A haircut, a change of address in a computer system, a 100 mile drive between two cities all take a predictable amount of time if done correctly and consistently. Call center processes should be no different.

Well defined processes *take as long as they take*, until and unless they are re-engineered. Unfortunately, the urgency of the ringing phone and the authority of Erlang blinds many managers to the issue at the heart of call center effectiveness. Agents are, in effect, continually being asked to "drive faster" - and the consequence is increased process variability.

All variability, not just call arrival times, will rapidly lower call center utilization, raise costs, and undermine the quality of customer service. The prime directive of any operations manager is to _manage_ variability and to run correct, consistent and capable processes.

Erlang's traffic engineering formulas only take into account variability in call arrival times but have no real management advice on every other potential source of variation. It is, in effect, a "no smoking" policy in a burning house.

THE TOTAL VARIABILITY PICTURE

Take a look at the Pollaczek-Kyntchin equation that describes the relationship between wait time, utilization and call handling variability. The three lines represent estimated average *wait* times with increasing levels of variability.

As Agents Get Busier....

Wait Time Exceeds Call Processing Time

Increased Variability Makes Things Much Worse!

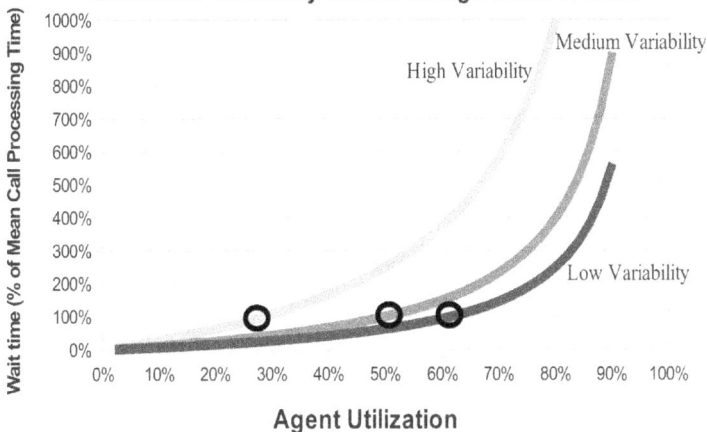

Erlang demonstrated this "hockey-stick" effect with arrival times but this pattern is true of *every* source of call handling variation in the call center operation. Unmanaged variability *eats your lunch.*

Managing call center variability is a multi-front initiative. A "holistic" approach embraces:

➤ Phone and computer issues

➤ Hiring and training policies

➤ Quality assurance methods

➤ Call Center metrics

➤ Coverage, scheduling and shift strategies

➤ Load forecasting methodologies

➤ Capacity planning

➤ Call-control scripts

➤ Proper roles and division of labor for supervisors, managers and *mission control* personnel

➤ Call Center *Express Lanes*

➤ *and more.*

EFFECTIVE CALL CENTER STRATEGY

*Reduce and Manage **all** sources of Variability. Design and Organize the Call Center in such a way that tactical managers have real-time options for quantifying and responding to change. The chief tool of the tactical manager is the ability to <u>re-deploy available resources</u> as needed.*

What Are The Odds you Can Use At Least One?

Management of variability is the unifying principle that enables the modern call center to improve performance, customer and employee satisfaction while lowering costs.

31: How Many Phone Lines Are Enough?

Conventional wisdom uses a calculation called Erlang-B to anticipate the likelihood of blocked calls. Of course, Erlang-B was devised over one hundred years ago. In that simpler time, there was no two-way and multi-party conferencing, no IVRs and no voice mail.

Still, the calculations give us a starting point for estimating line requirements. If we *reformulate Erlang-B in terms of line utilization*, we get a mathematical model that allows us to infer the call load *offered* from the *actual* line utilization.

A SIMPLIFIED EXAMPLE

Set aside call waiting, voice mail, and other modern call handling. Assume that you have a single incoming line that, when in use, rings BUSY to an outside caller.

If your average use of that line is 50%, it is reasonable to assume that *some* percentage of callers attempted their call while you were on the line. Those callers would receive a BUSY signal.

ADDING PHONE LINES

Now imagine a second *rollover* line. Many of the callers who would have first received a busy would now ring through on the second line. A smaller percentage would by chance call at times when **both** lines were in use. Well what about a total of 23 lines, the typical **T1**?

CALCULATIONS FOR A T1

Suppose the 23 lines in a T1 were in use an average of 65% of the time. Of course, *average* means sometimes the utilization is lower and sometimes higher.

Based on an average utilization of 65%, there will be small periods of time when all of the lines will be in use and periods when all lines are available. My first estimates based on Erlang-B suggest that 1% of callers will experience BUSY at this level of utilization.

More Than 1% of Callers Will Get a Busy Signal

If You have Too Few Phone Lines And Your Utilization Exceeds This Line

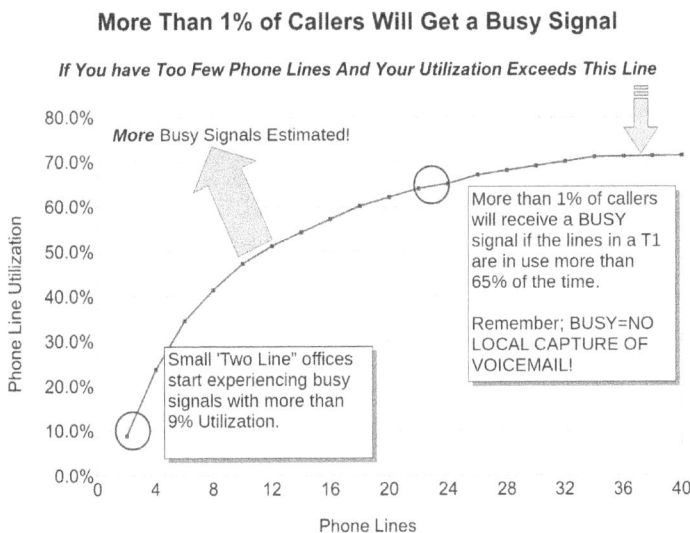

Remember that your in-house IVR needs phone lines. Your in-house voicemail requires phone lines. If your phone company cannot find available line capacity to *hand off* a call, it will return a BUSY signal to the caller, even in this modern era.

Don't forget to look at the telephone company side of telephone usage reporting. Calls that are never delivered may not even register in your telephone metrics and reporting systems.

One sly and unscrupulous call center manager finagled a large improvement in his service level statistics by simply unplugging one of their incoming T1s!

The reporting system could not see calls if they were not received by the company PBX; the sudden drop in call volume resulted in an instant *boost* in the call center's speed-of-answer scores.

CONCLUSION

Don't scrimp on incoming line services. In this age of SIP trunk technology and sophisticated call routing, an adequate number of incoming lines and alternate call destinations is affordable and it is possible to capture almost every incoming customer call. A 1% busy rate is last century's *low bar* standard.

32: Reason and Emotion

Perhaps our culture is overly influenced by old Star Trek reruns, but it is not *Reason versus Emotion*. It is Reason *and* Emotion! Unfortunately, many call center agents are *not* trained in this fine point of human psychology. In fact, agent orientation for call control and management often gets this distinction completely wrong.

In my agent training exercises, we use a simple 2x2 matrix to clear up any confusion on this issue. The *true* opposite of Emotional is *un*emotional. *Un*emotional behavior and speech is often described as *cold, colorless, uninviting* and *flat*. Emotional behavior is typically called *warm, colorful* and *energetic*.

Emotional and *un*emotional are true opposites and they make up one half of our 2x2 matrix. When *Reason* is added to the matrix, agents see that *Reason* can be both emotional and *un*emotional. To many, this is an enlightenment.

UNDERSTANDING CUSTOMERS

Some agents are reactive and responsive to customers who express strong emotion and some customers know it. They will feign emotion, if necessary, just to communicate the seriousness of a problem and the urgent need for resolution. *"The customer was really mad about the outage. I had better call my supervisor and my manager!"*

But, agents must also be coached to be responsive to the reasonable customer who does *not* show strong emotion.

Failure to do so just perpetuates the attitude that increasingly outrageous behavior is the only way to get a customer service organization to respond.

I have often heard agents call an *emotional* customer, *"irrational"*. That is a misconception. Perhaps the agents are confusing positive and negative emotional behavior, but either can be appropriate and rational under the right circumstances.

Agents need to train their ears to hear **Reason** *with and without an overlay of emotion*, and they must learn to distinguish Reason from its *true opposite*. A person who *acts rationally* is exercising their *capacity for Reason*. Rational customers show a grasp of immediate and abstract facts of reality. They know, for example, that airplanes cannot fly without pilots or fuel and they do *not* demand to take off without either.

An irrational customer's behavior may be cold and flat or they may be filled with emotion, but the message that their words and emotions convey will fly in the face of reality. Their confusion cannot be explained as simply being mistaken or misinformed. They will have notions that simply cannot be reconciled with reality. (*Agents are cautioned not to confuse reality with policy!*)

APPROPRIATE ACTION

In brief, there are four courses of action recommended by our 2X2 matrix. We must convey to the rational customer that we take every request seriously and then immediately demonstrate this with brisk action. We need to be calm, reassuring and empathetic to the emotional customer and we sometimes need to display a little emotion *on behalf of the* unemotional customer.

Listening skills are important and every caller is unique, but it is paradoxical that we often must mirror a *muted opposite* behavior to effectively communicate that we *get it. "I am quite upset with the billing errors on your account, and I appreciate your calm attitude Mr. Johnson. We will fix this error immediately and call or email you to confirm that the matter has been resolved."*

There are two courses of action for dealing with the irrational customer. The first is *grounding.* It is sometimes possible to bring an irrational person back in touch with reality. To persuade the irrational customer to exercise their powers of Reason, we *avoid* the abstract (*"your airline ticket contract says..."*) and focus in the immediate tangible facts that can form a common ground.

If it is not possible to establish a common ground with an irrational customer, the alternative is *containment.* The damage an irrational customer can do must be minimized. Company policy and circumstances dictate explicitly what actions are possible.

SUMMARY

In the Star Trek TV series, three principal characters were often used to characterize the Reason versus Emotion point of view. Mr Spock was the icon for Reason, but his demonstration of that power was typically limited to logical deductions and rationalism. Dr. McCoy was the caricature of emotion and the series glossed over the fact that Reason is the difference between life and death in the practice of medicine.

Thirty Seven Ideas For Business Operation Improvement*

In many ways, Star Trek's captain was a better portrayal of *Human Reason*. Dramatic criticisms aside, the captain was always in command of the facts. He visibly weighed values and risks and his actions were relevant, effective and moral. His emotions were in harmony with his circumstances. So may we be.

33: Cross Platform:The Key To Open Source

There was a time when almost all computer programs were *open source.* Programs were acquired in FORTRAN, COBOL, BASIC, PL/1, etc.

One could see each instruction typed by the programmer along with any comments. This transparency allowed *anyone* to follow and audit the programmer's thinking, and adapt or correct the software as needed.

Before these programs could be run, they were *compiled and linked,* merged with subroutines for file storage, printing, etc. These subroutines customized the program to a specific manufacturer's hardware and to a specific operating system. The end product was called a *binary* or *executable* program file.

Sometimes modifications to the source code were necessary, but if you could get the program to *compile* and *link* up with a machine's specific subroutines, then the *executable version* of the program was reusable on every other identical hardware/software system.

INTELLECTUAL PROPERTY ISSUES

Early entrepreneurs saw the enormous potential in software and began to wonder how they would protect their intellectual property.

The most common solution was to *close off* access to source code. Programmers' source code became *closed* or off limits to anyone other than the developers.

Software companies began to distribute executable, or *binary only,* copies of their program. A product became defined as an executable targeted at *one* kind of hardware and one *version* of an operating system.

These pre-compiled and pre-linked programs would only run on a specific hardware and operating system combination. A program that ran on an Apple computer would not run on a Digital Equipment Corporation mini-computer or an IBM PC and vice versa.

A BRIEF GOLDEN AGE

Without a doubt, closed source products like Windows and Microsoft Office gave birth to an incredible burst of industrial productivity. But along with the profitable rise of companies like Microsoft, the *closed source* approach began to breed systemic problems in the software industry.

Binary programs for a 1998 computer became obsolete by 2000 unless operating systems were bloated with extra code for *backwards compatibility.* Software upgrades became an expensive treadmill for consumers and Wall Street came to expect a *bump* in tech profits every two years.

Programmers who once worked for company **X** became a potential liability to company **Y**, tainted by their exposure to company **X** closed source trade secrets.

As businesses became increasingly dependent on Information Technology, the lack of transparency and the rise of security concerns caused business to wonder exactly what was *in* the software they paid so dearly for.

First and second tier tech support could no longer *look at the code* when a program exhibited questionable behavior. The help desk had no option but to treat each application as a complex *black box.*

When a sophisticated end user *did* discover a defect that could only be remedied by a programming change, *every customer waited* until the keeper of the source code *chose* to acknowledge and address the problem.

Instead of being able to shop in a software marketplace of competitive excellence, customers began to be *locked in* to a few big vendors for a host of logistical reasons stemming from the *binary only* approach to software.

Last, but not least, company lawyers became as important to the company's profitability as their programmers, and lawsuits between software houses seem almost as routine as new product announcements.

THE RETURN OF OPEN SOURCE

A significant number of technology professionals have patiently awaited the return of open source. Noting that authors do not publish books that must be *read to you*, they conclude that there are many ways for programmers to earn a living without resorting to code secrecy.

For years, the Open Source community has been refining software for web servers, email systems, desktop computing, PBX and telephony, CRM, ERP and more.

These software professionals earn their living by supporting, enhancing, and hosting Open Source software, by offering training and supported binaries, and occasionally by offering small delimited binary add-ons that remain *closed source* for a short period of time.

It is important here to note that open source is the opposite of *binary only*. High quality Open Source software is often *Cross Platform*. Open Source *plus* binaries for Windows, Linux, Apple, etc. is quite common.

Open Source is not *public domain*. Outright plagiarism is forbidden. Source code is protected by copyrights that identify authors and keep the source *open*.

Open Source licenses may also place restrictions on the programs use, including to what extent the code may be used in whole or in part for other programmers' projects.

However, just as lawyers may peruse public records and adapt the legal formulations of any peer to their own purposes, open source programmers freely benefit from the experience of *their* peers and from reviewing the programming work of others.

IS IT TIME FOR YOU TO TRY OPEN SOURCE?

Many people are tempted by Linux and the world of desktop open source but are a little afraid of making the leap. I can understand this. Unless 100% of your computer usage is based on web browsing, you leave a large comfort zone when you first leap into the cold waters of Linux based systems. The biggest hurdle always seems to be business email.

If your email client is Outlook Express, Windows Live Mail, or another lightweight email client, then you will have little difficulty transitioning to Thunderbird or Evolution. If you are the typical Microsoft Outlook/Outlook Exchange user, you may be a little panicked at the thought of leaving your most used application program behind.

Spreadsheets, Word Processing, and Presentation applications also serve to *lock in* many desktop users to the Microsoft Windows environment. For other users, niche programs from Intuit and Adobe make it almost impossible to make a 100% change to open source.

CROSS PLATFORM – A TRANSITION TO OPEN SOURCE

Users can be eased into the next generation of computing by migration to cross-platform applications.

A few *big name* closed source applications today run on Windows and Mac desktop, but there are many excellent Open Source applications that run on Windows, Mac and Linux. Some even support mobile platforms like Android, Windows Mobile and iPhone.

By gradually introducing, qualifying, and standardizing on cross-platform applications, desktop computer users will find themselves moving into a world of choice, a world where there is less to fear from the two year software upgrade cycle.

They will find themselves using applications with a longer useful life and with a world-wide user community.

GETTING STARTED – WINDOWS USERS ONLY!

For an easy start to Open Source for Windows users, I recommend just one download (an applications *suite*) and one critical first *cross platform* application.

Go to HTTP://PortableApps.com. Download and build their suite of applications onto a generous sized USB memory stick.

This single kit gives you a portable library of cross-platform, open source applications that will run on almost any Windows computer – provided that you can run programs from your computer's USB port.

The portable versions of these programs run without needing installation into the windows operating system. They leave little or no trace of themselves behind when the USB memory stick is removed.

The PortableApps suite includes: word processors, spreadsheets, email clients, Web browsers, games, music players, anti-spyware and anti-virus security tools and much more. It does NOT include my recommended alternative to Outlook, but the very popular and capable Thunderbird application is included.

A generous sized USB stick will allow you to store data as well as the application suite. You will be able to store a complete cross platform application suite and your personal files on the USB.

Cross platform means that you will be able to install native versions of these applications on other platforms. Should you wish to load the data files onto a Windows, Mac or Linux computer, native versions of these portable apps will be able to read and write the data files on the portable USB.

THE FIRST APPLICATION

I would recommend one application be your first to learn and use - *KeePass*. It keeps all of your passwords in an encrypted file under a single master password.

Native versions of *KeePass* are available for Windows, Mac, Linux, iPhone, Android and other smart phones. The KeePass data file can be opened, read, and usually modified by these cross-platform versions of the program – provided that you remember the one master password!

If you presently keep passwords in Outlook, text files, or on handwritten notes, migrate to *KeePass*. If you presently use another password vault product, give *KeePass* a try for the sake of its portability. Just be sure to keep a backup copy of the encrypted password data file – in case you lose your USB.

WHAT COMES NEXT?

It's your choice. Sample the LibreOffice Word Processor, Spreadsheet or Presentation tools. Experiment with their ability to read and save files that are compatible with Microsoft Office.

Manage your money with gnuCash. Browse the web with Firefox or Opera. Chat with friends through instant messenger clients. Scan your computer for spyware and virus programs... and more.

When you are ready, native versions of these programs are available to download and install as a part of your Windows desktop system. You can decide when and how much of your daily work load to transfer to these new applications.

TRUECRYPT

TrueCrypt is not part of the PortableApps suite but it is highly portable, and can be installed on the same USB memory stick as the PortableApps suite.

TrueCrypt creates an encrypted and password protected Drive (e.g. **F:**, **G:**, etc.). The encrypted drive appears as an ordinary but very large data file on the USB memory stick. If you make a habit of saving portable files on your TrueCrypt drive, this will offer some security if the USB device is ever misplaced.

Don't forget! All data security begins with physical security. If you put sensitive data on removable storage, Rule #2 is encrypt it. Rule #1 is to know where that storage device is at all times!

Since TrueCrypt temporarily adds a *plug and play* drive letter to the host Windows system, it does leave footprints that CSI computer skills can identify. However, in this day of sophisticated *key-loggers*, no public computer can ever be considered secure.

WHAT ABOUT EMAIL?

If you are an Outlook/Outlook Exchange user, this is surely one of the stickiest, *hard to leave* applications ever built. Technology managers and users both love and hate Outlook/Outlook Exchange.

There are Open Source alternatives, but the alternatives are not for everyone. Corporate email servers are often the interconnecting hub of many business processes. Change must be carefully planned with contingencies, pilot runs and due diligence.

My first preference for an Open Source Outlook/Exchange replacement is Zimbra. I would recommend that you first try Zimbra Desktop as a desktop email client. Like Outlook, it allows you to either download your email or synchronize email with a server that retains backup copies of undeleted messages.

Zimbra incorporates calendars, tasks, contacts and more. With the proper server, it offers shared calendars, shared contacts, shared project files and more. *Zimlets* are modular add-ons to Zimbra that extend the program's functionality.

Try the Zimbra desktop client with Google or Yahoo email first. It is easy to configure. Just enter your email address and password. Calendars and Contacts from the Google web site should synchronize with the desktop client and be available for off-line user. Google's email *tagging* system maps nicely into conventional email file folders within the Zimbra program.

Next, discover how easy it is to manage multiple email accounts with Zimbra. Add another gmail account, a POP or IMAP account or a Zimbra server account through a hosting company like HTTP://01.com.

A simple trial of two or three Zimbra client accounts on a hosted Zimbra server will let you compare and contrast the workgroup features of Zimbra with Outlook and Microsoft Exchange.

LINUX END GAME

When you find the majority of your computer tasks are satisfied with these cross-platform applications, you may want to consider transitioning to a Linux desktop environment.

Ubuntu is an excellent introduction to Linux. It is easy to install. You should choose the 64-bit version if your computer has more than 3GB of main memory. New versions of Ubuntu are released every six months.

Ubuntu has a mechanism similar to a smartphone *app store* and many of the programs in the PortableApps suite can be downloaded and installed as Ubuntu binaries with a mouse click. Some program installations are a bit more involved; you may need some help until you learn a few Linux user tricks.

As Windows users, once we learn our way around ZIP and EXE files, we sometimes take for granted that all computers will work in the same way. Linux is not harder but it is *different* and there is a learning curve to install programs that are not in the app library, or to install programs from source.

For those one or two Windows applications that you cannot currently leave behind, such as Quickbooks, I recommend VirtualBox OSE. This application is in the Ubuntu repository for *click and download* installation.

VirtualBox allows you to run a Windows Operating System within a window on your Linux Desktop machine. Although some will prefer a similar program from VMware, I have tried both and would need a compelling reason to use something other than VirtualBox OSE (Open Source Edition) in a desktop computer environment.

OEM copies of Windows XP are intended to be run on a single computer. Original retail copies of the operating system were more generously licensed. If you have a legal copy of XP, you can load it, build it, assign it a portion of main memory and run it inside a window on a Linux desktop computer.

As long as your copy of XP can be patched with the final security and feature updates from the Windows Update site, and as long as your Windows Applications are supported and run on XP – there is no reason to run later versions of the Windows operating system on Linux.

SUMMARY

Open Source is about availability of *source code*. Open Source means that the source code can be read, audited, modified and recompiled for a new platform without the legal *tripwires* of conventional software licenses..

With proprietary source distributed only in binary program form, there is generally only one company in the world that can modify or repair the application and they don't always choose to.

Skeptics often rhetorically ask, *"Who supports Open Source?"* I reply, *"Who supports Microsoft Frontpage? Where can I even buy it?"* With Open Source, there is someone on this earth that can modify, extend or repair the application even if the code is ten years old.

The re-usability of Open Source enables an IT strategy that lengthens the useful life of code. Binary only code with its two year upgrade cycle *becomes quickly obsolete.*

Open Source has the ability to lengthen technology life cycles, increase productivity, and lower the hardware, software and training costs of business technology. The time to try it is *now*!

34: Cause, Credit and Blame

Not every consequence must be filed under who takes credit and who is to blame. The reason some politicians insist on assigning credit or blame is simple. Every *opportunity* to assign credit and blame is a chance to advance personally or to demote their adversaries.

This *blame game* may be related to the psychology of the Internet Troll. Trolls are those who darken public forums, not to contribute or learn, but to score rhetorical victories. This behavior can also emerge in the corporate conference room, where it can be contagious.

Unchecked, one person can stir up a cry for the proverbial torches and pitchforks when things go wrong. That same person is typically the one overly concerned about receiving every ounce of credit when things go right.

If leadership thinking is poisoned by this flaw, then everyone who works for that manager is susceptible to this contagious error of thinking. This is why wise leaders focus first on *causes* of success and failure. They are generous with sharing credit and cautious with blame.

To be *fair* in one's dealings with peers and subordinates, one must always strive to see reality objectively. If you are clear in your thinking, you will see that there are things you can control, and know you can, and things you cannot control and know you can't.

A clear thinker is also wary of two potential errors. There are things you cannot control *but think you can* and things you can control *but think you can't*. (*Thank you, Dr. Charles Hobbs!*)

These principles go a long way towards establishing a framework for accountability that will enhance the harmony and cohesiveness of your team and their ability to work cooperatively and be productive together.

35: Personality and Character

Many people often confuse the concepts of personality and character. Past personal experience and reputation lead us to expect what an individual will likely do or say (*character*), and how they will do or say it (*personality*).

Since individuals have the ability to think and choose, there is always the possibility that they will surprise us and act *out of character*. Nevertheless, the concepts of character and personality are still valid.

Life is a sum and it requires consistent new behavior to change the cumulative direction of many past choices, *turn the ship* and establish a new character. The same thing can be said of organizations.

Instead of simply making more *tactical* decisions **in** character and at the margin, leadership has the power to **change** the character of an organization but this demands a change of *strategy*, a change of goals and a corresponding change of guiding principles appropriate to those goals.

36: Effective Process Management - Business Process Mapping

In the 60s and 70s, programmers were admonished to *flowchart* their programs before writing code. The flowchart was to be the first exhibit in a properly and completely documented program package. It was evidence that the work had been planned and that programmers had followed the plan.

From all accounts, compliance was spotty, to say the least. Despite psychological carrots and sticks, complete flowcharts of programs were never really made and used except, perhaps, by beginners and students. High-productivity programmers might sketch a flow for a particularly tricky bit of code but other techniques such as pseudo-code note-taking, story-boarding, and functional block diagrams were more common.

Flow Charting became commonplace only after programs were available that could grind out the obligatory *standards-compliant* diagram from *finished* source code. The Flow Chart era was driven by a well-intentioned notion, but was fatally flawed.

The flow-chart technique was simply not suitable to the task of helping the programmer think. It did not mentally group and simplify (*conceptualize*) the functions of the program in a way that was useful to the creative mind of the programmer.

Today, I fear that the specialty of Process Management is making a similar mistake with the current generation of Process Management mapping software. This software intends to flow chart business processes in the most minute detail - hoping to reduce the management of such processes to a matter of employee and customer obedience. (*"If we can just get everyone to follow our process..."*)

We then foster a culture where employees never question assumptions. A critical control knob is marked one to ten, and what does the obedient employee say? *"Really smart people placed it on setting four and told me to never touch it."* and, *"There cannot be a bug in the software, or a mistake in your account. Our programmers would have known."* (Sadly, these two quotes are excerpted from very true stories.)

Such an approach to process is *brittle*, not robust. It does not cope well with inevitable change. Some companies spend months or years attempting to portray the process realities they see in the corporate rear view mirror. The microscopically detailed process map inevitably lags behind the realities of work. Customers as well as employees are left feeling they have been given the one size fits all treatment.

To remedy this inflexibility, planners program the process with jack-in-the-box *triggers* - so called *business rules* that shift and route cases through systems like a fun-house car. *"I don't know why the computer won't let me add that feature to your account!"* the customer agent will say.

The system has been designed to be incomprehensible from the outside looking in and understandable only to the process mappers who have permission to look *under the hood.*

Thirty Seven Ideas For Business Operation Improvement*

Effective process management achieves consistency through understanding, not obedience. If there is a critical control knob, a critical time of day, or a critical phase of the moon, then we want to capture and organize that knowledge in such a way that that information can be shared and understood by every associate.

I would encourage you to take a very different approach to process mapping. At the highest level of detail, you must restrict yourself to describing the most essential ideas of the process (*verbs*), and its products (Incoming, Results, and By-Product *nouns*) on a single piece of paper/screen. Remember, you are not programming automation, you are preparing and organizing knowledge to be assimilated by a human being.

Break the process down into no more than five essential *action* ideas. (Each of these process ideas can be refined on a separate sheet of paper.) I use a functional block diagram - a dependency diagram to visualize these actions.

The dependency is not just causal or temporal. A precedent on a dependency diagram is that which must be *correct* for any action that follows to be deemed correct. In effect, we are documenting a conceptual chain - the assumptions that we must validate to conclude that a process is correct and not actions which by nature or schedule must precede others.

Although the currently popular methods *may* be effective at achieving some process consistency, we are striving for processes that are first and foremost *correct* to the limits of our understanding, and then *consistent* as an important *second but subordinate* virtue.

What Are The Odds you Can Use At Least One?

With this conceptual approach to process documentation, we look to associates not just for compliance, but for a certain kind of *gap analysis* that *expands* our understanding. By empowering a workforce to think about a process, we vastly multiply the number of minds who continually survey our process for gaps with reality - for evidence of things that don't fit.

One page functional block diagrams are a top-level organizing tool. Other supporting documentation is required to fully capture and share what is known about a correct, consistent and capable process. If you start with a proper dependency diagram, then you establish a conceptual context.

You create a *filing system* that will organize every piece of information you acquire. It will then function as a tool which will help you to *check your assumptions* when things change, or when new facts expose the gaps between your perfect process and reality.

Don't expect to absorb this notion by simply reading this article once. Skill and understanding of a conceptual approach to effective process documentation is developed in a manner similar to English composition *outlining* skills. Some of us sat through a semester and did not fully grasp the purpose and power of using an outline to organize an essay.

Give this method time. Look at your workforce. Do you have obedient employees, or employees than can think and contribute to the efficacy of your business processes? Let this alternative motivate you. After twenty years of practicing this technique, I continue to find it to be a rapid and effective method for operation improvement.

37: Automation Pitfall

The control knob was set on Position **4** and taped. "What does it do?" I asked a supervisor.

"Don't exactly know." he said. "It has something to do with the product thickness control system. Some pretty smart folks must have figured out that 4 was right. I was told not to touch it!"

If this sounds like your facility, let me tell you what comes next. In a month or a year, maintenance will finally remove this bit of technology and automation. They will say it is justified because no one uses it and that the continued maintenance costs should be saved now that times are tough.

Today, someone reaps praise for *saving* millions *by removing* process *enhancements* that *saved millions when they were installed* ten years ago.

I'm not just being cynical. There is a common, avoidable error that is often made in the implementation of technology and automation. Because of this error, the expected savings of technology may not materialize.

To understand and avoid this error we have to give ourselves a little background.

THE BUSINESS PROCESS

The difference between a bread making business and a guy with a bread-making machine is process knowledge.

What Are The Odds you Can Use At Least One?

Successful businesses have processes, intentional methods designed to correctly produce a particular product consistently. Processes can have a known capability, capacity, cost of quality and unit cost.

The guy with a bread-making machine may be able to turn the machine on and even produce a loaf of bread, but his initial methods are not necessarily intentional and designed. Too often, what the guy with a machine calls process is trial and error... and luck.

Within a work-center, a business process is an intentional, designed baseline plan for roles, stations, tasks and targets. It is the organized knowledge of who does what, where, when and *why.*

Many industries recognize that it is not the job of the day-to-day process manager to create tactical processes from scratch. In retail sales, specialty teams move through each location to *set* the store. In restaurant franchises, franchise schools and start-up crews help establish the business processes and pass along the process knowledge to management.

Process managers should be responsible for the correct and consistent operation of the business process and should contribute to systematic improvement. They are not responsible for its invention, or re-invention!

WHAT ADDED AUTOMATION CAN DO

Let's say that a particular process requires 128 tasks that must be done every hour of every day. With experience, processes are improved. The task list grows to, perhaps, 135 specific things that must be done.

149

Seven items are added to the task list because we learn additional things we should do to run the process correctly. They are tasks that become part of the definition of *correct* because they have economic benefit.

> *Each task may only increase utilization or reduce quality risks by a tiny but definite 0.1% but the return exceeds the cost.*

Only strategic re-engineering of a process *eliminates* tasks. New materials make new tools & technology possible. A strategic re-design of an operation may literally eliminate work and replace the process of 135 tasks with one that requires only 17.

For example: a key mechanical device consisting of windings, rotor, shaft and bearings may be replaced by *artificial muscle technology*. The issue of periodic motor-bearing inspection is now moot.

In the absence of a new strategic approach, technology and automation does is not eliminate tasks, *it consolidates them*. If the 135 tasks are initially performed by 135 employees, automation may allow the same 135 tasks to be performed by only 17 people!

Automation allows an individual to be (virtually) in many places at once. It may enable tasks to be performed faster, only when needed, or just in time. It may change the economic sweet spot of work and return. Thanks to automation, the original larger staff of 135 may be able to perform *1000 tasks* that each marginally benefit utilization, quality and capacity.

So, the new thickness control system that is *taped at position 4* may have been intended to enable one *knowledgeable* worker to perform 100 tasks and make 100 adjustments that keep the process optimized when temperature, humidity or other external factors fluctuate.

THE MISTAKE

The management mistake that undermines the potential of automation is the confusion of task consolidation with task elimination. Automation may change the inspection of a critical mechanical component. Instead of a greasy, hands-on task of visual inspection, we now inspect with an instrument and we ADD the task of certifying the instrumentation!

We haven't eliminated anything; we still have an *inspection* task. The requirement of a mechanical assessment is dictated by strategic engineering. Automation has transformed the task from one that takes four hours and requires *wrench* know-how, into two tasks that takes seconds, but may require *thermal sensor* know-how.

We compound the mistake by not educating our workforce about how these new tools work and the importance of the tasks these tools allow them to perform. We don't take into account the new tasks implied by automation - for example, the certification of instrumentation. When automation allows the workforce to be reduced, we often eliminate the very people who have some grasp of the role added automation plays in an improved process.

If we succomb to these automation pitfalls, then performance measures gradually deteriorate. Quality scores, utilization and unit costs gradually begin to trend in the wrong direction. The number of un-audited and un-maintained automation systems increases. Operators stop reading gauges because they no longer work, and all of our competitive advantage that was supposed to derive from *our people working smarter* gradually fades away.

Top management then asks, *"If we can't make automation work as a competitive advantage, and if we need 1000 workers to perform 1000 tasks; then where in the world can we find a price-competitive workforce?"*

CONCLUSION

In a modern business, it is unacceptable to have gauges, controls, computer reports metrics, and machine adjustments which are mysterious unknowns to the operations work force. It is an untenable position when operations have slipped into a mode where gauges and controls don't work and no one is convinced that it matters. The result is a slow creeping loss of competitiveness that many may not grasp until it is too late.

This mistake is avoided by retaining, organizing and communicating process knowledge. A business must never forget all of the specific operations tasks that brought them competitive success.

Management needs to recognize that automation is not the *silver bullet* that eliminates work. Automation adds tasks and *leverages* effort. When it comes to managing a process, there is more to think about when automation is added.

Our Management Philosophy

FIRST: THINK & COMMUNICATE CLEARLY

Practice and encourage the policy of only using words and acronyms you are prepared to define. You needn't be a surgeon to discuss *brain surgery*, but you should to be able to define *brain* and *surgery*. If it is true that you can´t effectively manage without measuring, then you surely can´t manage what you cannot define.

SECOND: BE DECISIVE

The time for action and the decision to act are two different things. The difference between Decisiveness and Impulsiveness is patient and prudent timing of action. Decisiveness is the ability to mentally adjudicate a matter so that it no longer consumes your most precious resource - your focus.

THIRD: DON'T BE A "BOTTLENECK"

Successful follow-through takes a network of key individuals and massively parallel and well organized activity. If you try to do everything yourself, then you will limit managed work to your personal ability to process information and make decisions.

FOURTH: HOLD PEOPLE ACCOUNTABLE FOR THINGS THEY CAN CONTROL

Properly apportion work and responsibility. An objective division of labor is based on product, process, decision-role and human factors. Holding people accountable for the wrong things is self-deceiving, self-defeating and the biggest destroyer of productivity and morale. Make sure you understand the difference between accountability and blame.

FIFTH: BUILD REAL PROCESSES

Processes are intentional methods of achieving repeatable results at a predictable cost. Many operations claim to have processes, but upon examination, they obviously don't. If every little undertaking is approached as a first-time initiative, then a company only achieves a fraction of its potential for productivity.

SIXTH: PAY ATTENTION, AND MAKE EVERY DAY A REAL DAY OF JOB EXPERIENCE

When we were young, we were told to *"pay attention in school"*. However, at any skill level, the essence of work is attention. Learn and encourage the policy of learning something new every day. Evaluate what you learn. Call a bad theory just that; not a *"good theory that doesn't work in practice"*.